Rose

(*Rosa*)

Herb of the Year 2012 ™

International Herb Association

Compiled & Edited by Susan Belsinger

The Herb of the Year ™

EVERY YEAR THE International Herb Association chooses an Herb of the Year ™ to highlight. Herbal organizations around the world work together with us to educate the public throughout the year.

Published by
International Herb Association
P.O. Box 5667
Jacksonville, Florida 32247-5667
www.iherb.org

Printed by
Litho Printers & Bindery
Cassville, Missouri 65625

This book is intended as an informational guide. The remedies, approaches and techniques described herein are meant to supplement, and not to be a substitute for professional medical care or treatment; please consult your health care provider.

The International Herb Association is a professional trade organization providing education, service and development for members engaged in all aspects of the herbal industry.

ISBN 978-1-4507-8836-6

*"Uniting Herb Professionals for Growth
Through Promotion and Education"*

*This book is dedicated to
our dear friend and herbal mentor
Thomas DeBaggio.*

Deep appreciation goes to our board members and board of trustees who generously give their time and energy to make the IHA what it is today.

Acknowledgements

FROM MY PERSPECTIVE, everything is coming up roses! Each year, the International Herb Association's Herb of the Year ™ book gets bigger and better. And *Rose, Herb of the Year 2012*™ is certainly no exception. This year's contributions are quite diverse and range from botany and cultivation to history and lore, from fragrance and flavor to recipes for the kitchen, bath, boudoir and apothecary. This is a wonderful compilation of researched topics, essays, literature and poetry, recipes, illustrations and photography featuring *Rosa*. On behalf of the IHA Board and Foundation, I would like to thank each and every contributor who helped to create this publication—a veritable bouquet of roses.

We are privileged to have an array of articles by Gert Coleman, Pat Crocker, Davy Dabney, Karen England, Kathleen Gips, Terry Hollembaek, Pat Kenny, Carol Little, Theresa Loe, Karen O'Brien, Dorene Petersen, Holly Shimizu, Ann Sprayregen, Skye Suter, Arthur Tucker, Tina Marie Wilcox, Robbi Will and Mike Shoup from the Antique Rose Emporium, and Betsy Williams.

Thanks to Lucia Bettler, Pat Crocker, Karen England, Deborah Hall, Terry Hollembaek, Pat Kenny, Jim Long, Holly Shimizu, Jane Taylor, Art Tucker, Kay Whitlock, and Tina Marie Wilcox for sharing their favorite roses.

There are excellent, experienced cooks among our recipe contributors: Pat Crocker, Karen England, Donna Frawley, Stephen Lee, Carol Little, Jim Long, Kiva Rose and Skye Suter—thanks to each one of you for sharing your recipes. Besides delectables for the kitchen, this year we have recipes for the apothecary and the bath and boudoir created by Davy Dabney, Donna Frawley, Carol Little, Marge Powell, and Andrea and Matthias Reisen as well as Dorene Petersen on the medicinal aspects of roses.

We are delighted to have such an impressive group of artists inspired by roses with illustrations by Adam Bridgewater, Pat Kenny and Skye Suter. The many photos throughout the book and on the cover were taken by Susan Belsinger, Pat Crocker, Karen England, Donna Frawley, Pat Kenny, Karen O'Brien, Dorene Petersen, Marge Powell, Andrea and Matthias Reisen, Kiva Rose, Robert Seidel, Holly Shimizu (courtesy of the United States Botanic Garden), and Lee Taylor.

My appreciation goes to Deborah Hall for her generous lending of books and her beautiful roses; to Pat Kenny for sharing her old books and her commitment to all things herbal; to Donna Frawley for organizing our annual conference, which led us down so many rose garden paths; to Tina Marie Wilcox for her continual support and for growing the roses for me to use at the Ozark Folk Center; to Robbi Will for her tour of the Antique Rose Emporium, answering my questions and allowing us to use the Antique Rose Care Guide; and to Kelly Farrell and Julie Cumberland for willingly letting me stage and shoot photos at their home.

Special thanks to my family for putting up with my recent distraction and obsession for roses.

Louanne Sargent and Karen O'Brien proofread this book from cover to cover and their expertise and sharp eyes helped to make this a much better publication—thank you both for your time. Karen is "in training" since she will be taking over editorship of next year's book, *Elderberry, Herb of the Year 2013*™.

It is always a pleasure to work with Heidi Lowe and Marty Jenkins at Litho Printers. Heidi is a professional with a great deal of patience who works magic with her design savvy and knowledge and love of typefaces. Kudos to Karen O'Brien for the large task of storing, processing, and shipping our HOY books. Our organization would not know what to do without our treasurer Marge Powell, for keeping us straight on so many matters.

This compilation by members and friends of the IHA is yet another collective work of art. They say it takes a village … and this collective is overflowing with rose-growing herb lovers. Here's to celebrating *Rose, Herb of the Year, 2012*. May your roses always flourish and be fragrant!

---S.B., Editor
November 2011

Table of Contents

'Pat Austin' roses at the Untited States Botanic Garden

Botany & Cultivation

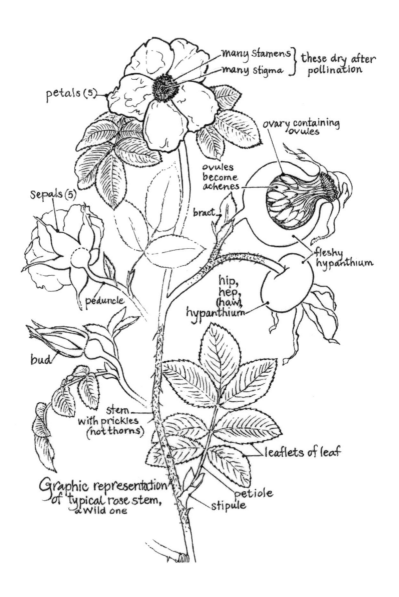

many stamens } these dry after
many stigma } pollination

petals (5)

ovary containing
ovules

ovules
become
achenes

Sepals (5)

bract

fleshy
hypanthium

hip,
hep,
(haw)
hypanthium

peduncle

bud

stem
with prickles
(not thorns)

leaflets of leaf

Graphic representation
of typical rose stem,
a wild one

petiole

stipule

Rosa

Arthur O. Tucker

Ed. Note: This chapter is updated and modified slightly from The Encyclopedia of Herbs co-authored by Arthur O. Tucker and Thomas DeBaggio, ed. by Francesco DeBaggio, published by Timber Press (2009).

Rosa: rō-zå
Family: Rosaceae
Growth form: shrubs 2 to 30 feet (61 cm to 9 m)
Hardiness: many routinely hardy to Zone 6
Light: full sun
Water: moist but not constantly wet
Soil: well-drained garden loam
Propagation: cuttings or grafts
Culinary use: salads, desserts
Craft use: potpourri, sachets, beads
Landscape use: shrubbery or rear of herb border
French: *rosier*
German: *Rose*
Dutch: *roos*
Italian: *rosa*
Spanish: *rosa, gavanzo, escaramujo*
Portuguese: *roseira*
Swedish: *ros*
Russian: *rosa*
Chinese: *ch'iang-wei, mei-kuei*
Japanese: *bara*
Arabic: *ward(a)*

GERTRUDE STEIN'S "A rose is a rose is a rose is a rose" strikes us as pitifully naive when you consider that the genus *Rosa* includes about 100 species of the temperate regions to tropical mountains and thousands of different named cultivars. The genus *Rosa* derives its name from the Latin, *rosa,* in turn from the Greek, *rhodon,* which, in turn, was derived the original Indo-European root-word, *ward,* still retained in the Arabic.

As implied from such an ancient Indo-European origin of the name, roses have been cultivated since ancient times; we find, for example, the depiction of what may be *R. gallica* in the House of Frescoes at Knossos dated to around 1400 B.C. Roses have enthralled humans for their beauty of form and scent down through the ages, and today we use rose petals for perfumes, cosmetics, and even salads, while the fruits, known as hips, are high in vitamin C with a tomato-like taste. Roses have long symbolized romance, and we find special pleasure and meaning in being able to grow, touch, and inhale the fragrance of the same rose that grandmother grew in West Virginia or Napoleon's Josephine grew at Malmaison.

The choice of a rose cultivar for its beauty and usefulness is an individual choice, but the nursery's methods of producing roses should be an important consideration as well. Roses sold today in North America and Europe are usually budded upon one of three different rootstocks, *R. canina, R. multiflora* Thunb., or 'Dr. Huey,' but some companies sell plants grown on their own roots ("own-root roses"). There are advantages and disadvantages to both methods. Generally, most heritage roses perform better with their own roots, but modern hybrids such as teas and floribundas, whose own roots tend to be weak, do better grafted to a more vigorous rootstock.

Some own-root roses often produce shoots from their own roots called suckers, especially if they have *R. gallica* ancestry; these suckers can be as troublesome as spreading mints and as difficult to manage. 'Dr. Huey' rootstock is fine for the sandy, alkaline soils of California and Texas, but for the acid soils of the northeastern United States, either *R. canina* or *R. multiflora* is preferred. For Florida and other subtropical areas, *R. xfortuniana* Lindl. is a must as a rootstock because of the combination of heat and nematodes.

The choice of the rootstock is almost as important as the grafted scion, and if the commercial company which sells the rose you desire does not give that information in their catalog, write or call them.

Also look for grading of the budded roses and buy only grade 1 to 1 1/2; these are the top grades awarded to plants with more canes and higher quality. An indication of a really good company is authentication that their budwood and rootstock have been indexed as virus-free. Expect, even with the best of companies, some misidentification, and if the company does not admit fault or refer you to a source for authentication, you may wish to look for another source.

Most roses do best in deep, fertile, moist but well-drained soils with a pH of 5.5 to 6.5; a position that provides full sun and good air circulation helps reduce disease and insects. The choice of species or cultivar (as well as your climate) will dictate spacing. If rooting of the scion is desired, plant the bud union about 2 to 3 inches (5 to 8 cm) below the soil level; otherwise, be sure that the bud union sets above the soil level. Some gardeners prefer fall-planting to give the roots extra time to establish themselves, but we have found that in Zone 7 and north, some winters will be so cold that the fall-planted roses will not survive.

Do not fertilize newly planted roses; wait four to six weeks for the plants to become established. Authorities do not agree on the type of fertilizer or the rate, only that roses are heavy feeders. We recommend yearly feedings of about a cupful of 5-10-5 fertilizer per established rose bush sprinkled in a circle around the base, supplemented with monthly feedings of fish emulsion, manure tea, or other organic sources of nutrients for maximum growth. Robust roses, such as 'Gardenia,' which puts out 40-foot canes even on poor soil, require additional fertilizer. Do not expect typical blossoms of a species or cultivar until the second year after planting. The blooms of the first year are smaller and sparser than are typical.

Many of the heritage roses are easily propagated by cuttings. Those that don't root easily from cuttings, such as the roses with heavy R. gallica ancestry, produce suckers, which are easily transplanted. Many people swear on pencil-sized green cuttings taken in the fall, but we have had good success with "heel" cuttings of blooming stalks. Cuttings taken at the time of flowering also guarantee proper labeling. The cleanliness, temperature, and humidity of the rooting chamber are of primary importance; rooting media that suffers from fungi contamination, high temperatures, or low humidity guarantees failure.

To prepare a spring rose cutting, choose a healthy blooming side shoot with at least three good terminal leaves. Rip the side branch off in a quick downward movement, removing some of the tissue of the main stem. Dip the cutting in rooting hormone and treat as advised in the propagation chapter.

We have found that a well-drained rooting medium of 50 percent perlite and 50 percent clay frit (baked cat litter) with clean mason jars and semi-shade work very well for small batches of rose cuttings; for larger volumes of roses, you may want to experiment with mist systems. For budding and other methods of propagation of roses, please see the books and articles cited in the bibliography.

The worst rose pests are thrips, leaf hoppers, rose slugs, and Japanese beetles. The first three can be controlled by spraying a dormant oil in early spring when you have twenty-four hours of above-freezing temperatures but before the buds have begun to burst. Japanese beetles can be controlled by strains of *Bacillus thuringiensis* applied to the adjacent lawns. If you use the Japanese beetle traps that have sex attractants and/or rose oil, be sure to place the trap far away from the roses and empty the traps often; placing the traps near the roses will guarantee that they are eaten.

Black spot and mildew are the most common diseases, and various claims of success have been made for sprays of baking soda (3 tablespoons per gallon of water) applied with an insecticidal soap (5 tablespoons per gallon water) or summer horticultural oil. Baking soda sprays must be reapplied after each heavy rain, and avoid overhead watering.

Picking rose petals is extremely labor-intensive. Pickers in New Zealand do not exceed 13.2 pounds per hour (6 kg/hr), but the average is 6.6 pounds per hour (3 kg/hr). At 0.09 to 0.18 ounce per flower (2.5 to 5.0 g/flower), this represents 91 to 181 flowers per pound (200 to 400 flowers/kg). A report from New Zealand indicates that *R. damascena* 'Trigintipetala' produced 12.3 pounds (5.6 kg) of flowers per plant during the third flowering season, for a total flower yield of 4.10 tons per acre (9.2 t/ha) at a density of 668 plants per acre (1650 plants/ha).

Either yields in New Zealand are exceptional, their plants are misidentified, or the decimal has been moved because in Delaware we only found 0.57 pounds (0.26 kg) of flowers per plant for authentic 'Trigintipetala' and 0.68 pounds (0.31 kg) of flowers per plant for 'Prof. Émile Perrot.' Typically, after picking, the rose petals are spread over cool concrete floors in the shade, where the rose petals may continue to produce rose scent, until they can be distilled.

The distillation of rose petals is unique in a number of aspects. The essential oil of most herbs can be steam-distilled by passing steam over the leaves, but rose petals "glop together" under steam to form an impenetrable mass. Hence, the best method to distill the essential oil from rose petals is water distillation; the rose petals are placed in a distillation unit, often a copper still, often with salty water, and then boiled. The heating drives off the steam and the volatile components that are condensed by a cold-water condenser.

The resulting product in most other plants is an oil, but in the case of rose petals, many plant waxes (paraffins) are also distilled, resulting in a waxy, oily product called an "attar" or "otto" (derived from the Arabic 'itr, meaning "perfume" or "essence"). The water contains many water-soluble components, particularly beta-phenylethanol, and this rose water is marketed for use in cosmetics or food. Rose petals may also be extracted with petroleum ether, producing a yellow-colored, waxy "concrète." Extraction of the odoriferous principles into ethyl alcohol, leaving behind the yellow pigments and waxes, produces an "absolute from concrète."

The typical rose scent is due to a simple water-soluble alcohol, beta-phenylethanol, and three monoterpenic oil-soluble alcohols, geraniol, nerol, and citronellol. The acetate esters of these alcohols are also rose-scented but of a slightly different fragrance. The clove-scented eugenol and methyl eugenol provide spiciness, while ionones give hints of violets. The relative concentrations of these chemicals determine the final odor. The attar may also be characterized by various waxes, such as nonadecane, eicosane, and heneicosae, but these are essentially odorless.

All of the following old roses, unfortunately, flower only once in spring. The fruit of some species, such as *R. canina* and *R. rugosa*, are large and red. These "hips," as the fruit is called, softened by the first heavy frost, have a tomato-like taste and are rich in vitamin C (ascorbic acid) and especially good prepared as conserves and jams with cream cheese for tea cakes. Under ideal conditions, rose hips may have 0.5 percent vitamin C. However, vitamin workers have reported asthma-like symptoms induced by inhalation of powdered rose hips.

In our discussion we have included seven basic rose species and ancient hybrids which have utility in the herb garden. Many cultivars, particularly those designated as "heritage" roses, could also be recommended, but remain beyond the scope of this book.

The literature on roses is voluminous: for a survey of this literature, we recommend Keith Stock's *Rose Books*. Gerd Krüssmann's encyclopedic *The Complete Book of Roses* provides a general history and guide through the complex evolution of roses. For descriptions and dates of cultivars, Thomas Cairn's *Modern Roses XI* is a good introduction. For color pictures of the species and heritage roses, we recommend, in particular, Peter Beales's *Classic Roses*, Trevor Griffiths's *The Book of Old Roses* and *The Book of Classic Old Roses*, and Roger Phillips and Martyn Rix's *Roses*. Look for books on rose culture in your region, such as Liz Druitt and G. Michael Shoup's *Landscaping with Antique Roses*, which is great for the Deep South.

White Rose

Rosa alba
rō-zǎ ǎl-bǎ

THE WHITE ROSE is unknown outside of cultivation and has an unknown pedigree. The white rose has clean, white petals with bluish green foliage and a wonderful old-rose scent; it is typified by a Linnaean specimen with nine petals. This is var. *alba*, sometimes incorrectly designated as 'Semi-Plena'; it may bear up to twelve petals. *Rosa alba* var. *alba* has been called the "York" rose because it was chosen by Edward IV (reigned 1461-1470) as a symbol of the House of York. Another cultivar is 'Suaveolens,' the white rose of the perfumers since before 1899, with twelve to sixteen petals. 'Suaveolens' is typically used as a windbreak for the damask rose fields in Bulgaria, and the petals are also harvested for the commercial attar. 'Maxima,' with forty-four to fifty-one petals, was the rose of the Jacobites, chosen by the supporters of the House of Stuart after James II lost his throne in 1688. 'Maxima' predates 1400 and was often pictured in fifteenth-century paintings.

Important Chemistry: The attars of 'Suaveolens' and 'Maxima' are very similar, with 32 to 34 percent geraniol and 18 percent nerol.

Dog Rose

Rosa canina
rō-zå kå-nī-nå

THE DOG ROSE or dog hip is typically used as a rootstock for grafting hybrids, particularly by nurseries in England, and it is frequently naturalized in North America. This is a large shrub to 8 feet (2.4 m). The flowers are single and pink; the hips (fruits) are orange-red, large, tasty, and high in vitamin C. The seeds yield an oil rich in *trans*-retanoic acid and are potentially useful for cosmetics.

Cabbage Rose

Rosa centifolia
rō-zå sĕn-tĭ-fō-lĭ-å
French: *rose de Mai, rose pâle, centfeuilles, rose de Provins*
German: *Zentifolien-Rose, Centifolien-Rose, Provence Rose*
Dutch: *centifolia roos, Provence roos*
Italian: *rosa centofoglie*
Spanish: *rosa centifolia, rosa de cien hojas, rosa común*

CABBAGE ROSE, OR *rose de Mai* in French, may date from ancient times, but it definitely appeared in the form 'Maxima' from Dutch nurseries in the sixteenth century. 'Maxima' is difficult to locate today, and some modern nurseries pawn off other cultivars that do not match the 'Maxima' pictured in early Dutch paintings. The true 'Maxima' looks like a small, pink cabbage, as the name implies. While desirable for form, color, and texture, the true cabbage roses tend to be rather weak plants.

Rosa centifolia, translated as the hundred-leaved (petaled) rose, gave rise to many cultivars in Dutch and French nurseries. Today some nurseries still offer 'Bullata' (c. 1801), the cabbage-leaved cabbage rose, with red-tinged leaves that are crinkled like a those of a cabbage. The cabbage rose is particularly noted for sporting in the past to the moss roses; these roses have a distinctive pine-scented mossiness on the flower stem, hypanthium, and sepals. The most distinctive early moss is 'Crested Moss' ('Chapeau de Napoléon, 1827). These cultivars also have that full, cabbagy form and old-rose scent typical of the true cabbage rose in addition to the moss.

The rose water of *R. centifolia* is listed as GRAS at 100 ppm. Rose oil from Morocco, reputedly *R. centifolia*, was found to have anticonflict effects from the content of beta-phenylethanol and citronellol.

Important Chemistry: The attar of 'Crested Moss' petals is dominated by 34 percent geraniol and 18 percent nerol. Oil from Morocco, supposedly *R. centifolia*, has 34 percent citronellol, 15 percent nonadecane, and 14 percent geraniol.

Summer Damask Rose

Rosa damascena
rō-zå dăm-å-sē-nå
French: *rose de Damas*
German: *Damaszener Rose*
Dutch: *damast roos*
Spanish: *rosa damascene*

THE SCIENTIFIC NAME of *Rosa damascena*, the summer damask rose, was first published by Jean Herrmann in his *Dissertatio Inauguralis Botanico-Medica de Rosa* in 1762. However, Herrmann's rose is not the damask rose we know, but an unidentified hybrid. Six years after Herrmann's description was published, Philip Miller published *R. damascena* for the rose that we grow today. Because Herrmann's prior use of this name takes precedence under the International Code of Botanical Nomenclature, the correct name of today's damask rose is actually unknown, but this is only one of many instances of confusion concerning the correct identity of roses. We use *R. damascena* here simply because no other name is currently available and generally understood. The damask rose may be derived from hybridization of *R. moschata* Herrm.,*R. gallica,* and *R. fedtschenkoana* Regel, but futher studies are need to confirm this.

The rose commercially cultivated in Kazanlik Valley of Bulgaria is usually listed in rose books as 'Trigintipetala,' a name first published by G. Dieck in 1889. This cultivar has become thoroughly confused in the nursery trade with 'Prof. Émile Perrot,' which was gathered from commercial fields in Iran and introduced by the rosarian Turbat in 1931. 'Prof. Émile Perrot' is the cultivar offered as 'Trigintipetala' by American, Canadian, and British nurseries; one leading American heritage-rose nursery even has the audacity to offer 'Alika' of 1906 as 'Trigintipetala'. A rose similar to 'Trigintipetala' is 'Gloire de Guilan,' which was gathered from commercial fields in the Caspian provinces of Iran by Nancy Lindsay and introduced by the Hilling, a British rose nursery, in 1949. All these damask roses bear double flowers, usually pink, with typical damask scent.

'York and Lancaster' ('Versicolor,' 'Variegata') is called the Tudor rose and supposedly originated about the time of Henry VII when he ascended the throne in 1485; this story may be apocryphal because the rose can be dated with certainty only to the description of Clusius in 1601. The petals are usually white but sometimes streaked light pink, thereby uniting in a floral emblem the Houses of York and Lancaster (see *R. alba* var. *alba* above and *R. gallica* 'Officinalis' below, also Shakespeare's *King Henry VI*, part 1, act 1, scene 4, when Henry VII marries his cousin, Elizabeth of York).

The attar of *R. damascena* is listed as GRAS at 0.01 to 15 ppm. The essential oil is antibacterial. The tea made from the petals is rich in antioxidants.

Important Chemistry: The commercial Bulgarian attar is dominated by 33 to 36 percent citronellol, 16 to 26 percent geraniol, and 5 to 14 percent nonadecane. Iranian oil is rich in 15 to 47 percent citronellol, 0 to 40 percent nonadecane, 0 to 19 percent docosane, 0 to 19 percent disiloxane, 0 to 18 percent geraniol, 0 to 18 percent heneicosane. Indian oil is rich in 15 to 36 percent geraniol, 12 to 36 percent citronellol, and trace to 25 percent nonadecane. Chinese oil is rich in 31 to 44 percent citronellol, 16 to 22 percent geraniol, and 2 to 17 percent nonadecane. Gülbirlik rose oil from Turkey has 31 to 44 percent citronellol, 8 to 15 percent nonadecane, and 9 to 14 percent geraniol. Turkish absolute is rich in 50 to 86 percent beta-phenylethanol. The attar of 'York and Lancaster' is dominated by 25 percent geranyl acetate plus citronellol, 17 percent geraniol, and 11 percent heneicosane. The attar of 'Triginti-petala' is dominated by 19 percent nonadecane, 15 percent geranyl acetate plus citronellol, 14 percent geraniol, and 11 percent heneicosane. The attar of 'Prof. Émile Perrot' is dominated by 21 percent geraniol, 19 percent geranyl acetate plus citronellol, and 13 percent nonadecane. The attar of 'Gloire de Guilan' is dominated by 33 percent geraniol and 12 percent nonadecane.

French Rose

Rosa gallica
rō-zå gǎl-lǐ-kå
French: *rose rouge*
German: *Gallische Rose*
Dutch: *rode franse roos*
Spanish: *rosa frances*

THE FRENCH OR Provins rose is usually cultivated as the semidouble, cherry pink cultivar 'Officinalis,' the apothecary's rose. 'Officinalis' dates to about 1240 and was the red rose of the House of Lancaster, chosen by Edmund, Earl of Lancaster in 1277. 'Officinalis' was the source of rose water as prepared in Provins, France. 'Versicolor' ('Rosamundi'), a striped version of 'Officinalis', has been sometimes ascribed to the "Fayre Rosamonde," the mistress of King Henry II of England, who died about 1176, but this rose can be dated with authority only to the description by L'Obel in 1581.

Rosa gallica 'Officinalis,' sometimes called the "red damask," was often pictured in paintings of the Virgin Mary, along with R. *alba* 'Maxima.' The apothecary's rose is a vigorous shrub to about 2.5 feet (0.8 m), but it sets out suckers like crazy from its own roots. The petals of 'Officinalis' retain their color nicely on drying and are thus good for potpourri. The petals are also reputed to retain their fragrance when dried, but we have not found any scientific proof for this tale.

Important Chemistry: The attar of 'Officinalis' is dominated by 17 percent nonadecane, 17 percent geraniol, and 12 percent nerol.

Eglantine

Rosa rubiginosa
rō-zå rŭ-bĭg-ĭ-nō-så

THE EGLANTINE OR sweet briar, known in French as églantier, has apple-scented young leaves. Except for the incense rose (R. primula Boulenger), with sandalwood-scented leaves, this is a rather unique characteristic among roses. It is full of prickles with single, pink roses and grows to about 8 feet (2.4 m) in height. The eglantine was important in the Penzance hybrids, such as 'Lord Penzance' of 1894, with apple-scented young leaves and single, coppery pink flowers.

Rugosa Rose

Rosa rugosa
rō-zå rŭ-gōs-å

THE RUGOSA OR ramanas rose is worth growing, not only for its large, red hips rich in vitamin C, but also because the curly, green foliage of this rose is rarely troubled by mildew or blackspot. The stems are coated with many fine green to brown prickles. Some hybrids of this rose, such as 'Hansa' (1905) have fine, damask rose-like odors besides good form and color. If you are interested in this species and its progeny, we recommend Suzanne Verrier's book *Rosa Rugosa*. Aqueous and ethanol extracts of dried ramanas rose flowers have been shown to have human immunodeficiency virus type 1 reverse transcriptase inhibitory activity.

Important Chemistry: The attar of rugosa rose petals is dominated by 31 to 38 percent beta-phenylethanol, trace to 29 percent citronellol, 0 to 19 percent geranyl formate, trace to 14 percent nerol, and 6 to 14 percent geraniol.

Botanical Description

NOTE: *A* KEY *has been omitted for two reasons. First, a key would not be useful unless the thousands of cultivars could be included. Secondly, while rose books continue to designate cultivars, such as 'Mme. Hardy,' as pure species, most roses are hybrids ('Mme. Hardy' is probably a damask × cabbage hybrid, not a pure damask rose).*

R. alba L., Sp. pl. 492. 1753.
Native country: The white rose is not known outside cultivation.
General habit: The white rose is a deciduous shrub to 2 m.
Leaves: Leaves are divided into five leaflets, 2 to 6 cm long, broad-elliptic or egg-shaped, toothed, hairy beneath.
Flowers: Flowers are semidouble to double, white.
Fruits/Seeds: Fruit is oblong-egg-shaped, red.

R. canina L., Sp. pl. 491. 1753.
Native country: The dog rose is native to Europe.
General habit: The dog rose is a deciduous shrub with green stems to 2.4 m.
Leaves: Leaves are divided into five to seven leaflets, 15 to 40 x 12 to 20 mm, egg-shaped or ellipse-shaped, toothed or doubly toothed, smooth and lacking in glands, dark to blue-green, shining or dull above.
Flowers: Flowers have 15 to 25 mm petals, pink to white.
Fruits/Seeds: Fruit is globose, ovoid, or ellipse-shaped, smooth, red.

R. centifolia L., Sp. pl. 491. 1753.

Native country: The cabbage rose is not known outside cultivation.

General habit: The cabbage rose is a deciduous shrub to 2 m.

Leaves: Leaves are divided into five leaflets, hairy on both sides or only beneath, toothed.

Flowers: Flowers are very double, pink.

Fruits/Seeds: Fruit is ellipsoid to almost globose.

R. damascena Mill., Gard. Dict. ed. 8. 1768.

Native country: The damask rose is not known outside cultivation.

General habit: The damask rose is a deciduous shrub to 2 m with numerous stout prickles.

Leaves: Leaves are divided into five to seven leaflets, egg-shaped to oblong-egg-shaped, toothed, smooth above, more or less hairy beneath.

Flowers: Flowers are double, pink.

Fruits/Seeds: Fruit is almost egg-shaped, hairy, red.

R. gallica L., Sp. pl. 492. 1753.

Native country: The French rose is native to southern and central Europe.

General habit: The French rose is a deciduous shrub, 0.4 to 0.8 m high, forming large patches.

Leaves: Leaves are divided into three to seven leaflets, 20 to 60 x 18 to 30 mm, leathery, almost globe-shaped to egg-shaped, rounded at the apex, usually doubly toothed, dull bluish-green and smooth above, paler, hairy, and glandular below.

Flowers: Solitary flowers, rarely two to four per stalk, are 6 to 9 cm in diameter, deep pink.

Fruits/Seeds: Fruit is globose to spindle-shaped, densely glandular hairy, bright red.

R. rubiginosa L., Mant. pl. 2:564. 1771 (*R. eglanteria* L.).

Native country: The eglantine is native to most of Europe.

General habit: The eglantine is a deciduous shrub to 3 m.

Leaves: Leaves are divided into five to seven leaflets, 10 to 25 x 8 to 15 mm, almost orbicular to egg-shaped, doubly toothed, smooth or hairy above, usually hairy and more or less glandular beneath.

Flowers: Flower has 8 to 15 mm petals, deep pink.

Fruits/Seeds: Fruit is almost globe-shaped, ovoid, or ellipse-shaped, smooth or glandular hairy, bright red.

R. rugosa Thunb., Fl. jap. 213. 1784.
Native country: The rugosa rose is native to China and Japan.
General habit: The rugosa rose is a deciduous shrub to 2 m, densely bristly and prickly.
Leaves: Leaves are divided into five to nine leaflets, 2 to 5 cm long, slightly waxy, wrinkled, lustrous, dark green, smooth above, hairy beneath.
Flowers: Flowers are single, cherry pink to purple to white.
Fruits/Seeds: Fruit is depressed globe-shaped, smooth, brick-red.

Sources

Antonelli, A., et al. 1997. Characterization of 24 old garden roses from their volatile compositions. *J. Agric. Food Chem.* 45: 4435-4439.

Aydinli, M., and M. Tuta. 2003. Production of rose absolute from rose concrete. *Flavour Fragrance J.* 28: 26-31.

Azimi, M., and R. J. Bisgrove. 1975. Rooting of hardwood cuttings of rose rootstocks and cultivars. *Exp. Hort.* 27: 22-27.

Babu, K. G. D., et al. 2002. Essential oil composition of damask rose (*Rosa damascena* Mill.) distilled under different pressures and temperatures. *Flavour Fragrance J.* 17: 136-140.

Balinova-Tsvetkova, A. 1997. On the extraction of *Rosa damascena* Miller. In *Essential oils: Basic and Applied Research.* Ed. Ch. Franz et al. Carol Stream, Illinois: Allured Publ. Co. 300-303.

Baser, K. H. C., et al. 2003. Turkish rose research: Recent results. *Perfumer Flavor* 28(2): 34-42.

Basim, E., and H. Basim. 2003. Antibacterial activity of *Rosa damascena* essential oil. *Fitoterapia* 74: 394-396.

Baydar, H., and N. G. Baydar. 2005. The effects of harvest date, fermentation, duration and Tween 20 treatment on essential oil content and composition of industrial oil rose (*Rosa damascena* Mill.). *Industr. Crops Prod.* 21: 251-255.

Beales, P. 1985. *Classic Roses.* New York: Holt, Rinehart and Winston.

Bruneau, A., et al. 2007. Phylogenetic relationships in the genus *Rosa:* New evidence from chloroplast DNA sequences and an appraisal of current knowledge. *Syst. Bot.* 32: 366-378.

Caissard, J.-C., et al. 2006. Chemical and histochemical analysis of 'Quatre Saisons Blanc Mousseaux', a moss rose of the *Rosa × damascena* group. *Ann. Bot.* 97: 231-238.

Cao, Y.-l., et al. 1996. Vitamin contents in the hips of 38 species of *Rosa* and their relation to division of sections. *Acta Bot. Sin.* 38: 822-827.

Concha, J., et al. 2006. Effect of rosehip extraction process on oil and defatted meal physicochemical properties. *J. Amer. Oil Chem. Soc.* 83: 771-775.

Cairns, R., ed. 2000. *Modern roses XI.* San Diego: Acad. Press.

Dobson, H. E. M., et al. 1990. Differences in fragrance chemistry between flower parts of *Rosa rugosa* Thunb. (Rosaceae). *Israel J. Bot.* 39: 143-156.

Druitt, L., and G. M. Shoup. 1992. *Landscaping with Antique Roses.* Newtown, Connecticut: Taunton Press.

Eikani, M. H., et al. 2005. Recovery of water-soluble constituents of rose oil using simultaneous distilaltion-extraction. *Flavour Fragrance J.* 20: 555-558.

Ercisli, S. 2005. Rose (Rosa spp.) germplasm resources of Turkey. *Gen. Resources Crop,. Evol.* 52: 787-795.

Fu, M., et al. 2006. Compounds from rose (*Rosa rugosa*) flowers with human immunodeficiency virus type 1 reverse transcriptase inhibitory activity. *J. Pharm. Pharmacol.* 58: 1275-1280.

Griffiths, T. 1984. *The Book of Old Roses.* London: Mermaid Books.

———. 1987. *The Book of Classic Old Roses.* London: Michael Jackson.

Gudin, S. 2000. Rose: Genetics and breeding. *Pl. Breeding Rev.* 17: 159-189.

Gupta, R., et al. 2000. Composition of flower essential oil of *Rosa damascena* and *Rosa indica* grown in Lucknow. *J. Med. Aromatic Pl. Sci.* 22-23: 9-12.

Hayward, M. R. 1997. The roses of Taif. *Saudi Aramco World* 48(6): 2-9.

Illés, V., et al. 1997. Extraction of hiprose fruit by supercritical CO_2 and propane. *J. Supercritical Fluids* 10: 209-218.

Iwata, H., et al. 2000. Triparental origin of damask roses. *Gene* 259: 53-59.

Jan, C. H., et al. 1999. Rose germplasm analysis with RAPD markers. *HortScience* 34: 341-345.

Jeremias, C. G. 1979. *Rooting rose cuttings.* Amer. Rose Annual 64: 91-108.

Jirovetz, L., et al. 2002. Comparaive investigations of essential oils and their

SPME headspace volatiles of *Rosa damascena* from Bulgaria and *Rosa centifolia* from Morocco using GC-FID, GC-MS and olfactometry. *J. Essential Oil-Bearing Pl.* 5: 111-121.

_____, et al. 2005. Solid phase microextrction/gas chromatographic and olfactory analysis of the scent and fixative properties of the essential oil of *Rosa damascena* L. from China. *Flavour Fragrance J.* 20: 7-12.

Klástersky, I. 1968. *Rosa. In Flora Europaea. Vol. 2.* Ed. T. G. Tutin et al. Cambridge Univ. Press. 25-32.

Knapp, H., et al. 1998. (S)-3,7-Dimethyl-5-octene-1,7-diol and related oxygenated monoterpenoids form petals *of Rosa damascena* Mill. *J. Agric. Food Chem.* 46: 1966-1970.

Koopman, W. J. M., et al.,. 2008. AFLP markers as a tool to reconstruct complex relationships: A case study in *Rosa* (Rosaceae). *Amer. J. Bot.* 95: 353-366.

Kovacheva, N, et al. 2006. Study on the morphological characteristics and essential oil constituents Bulgarian oil-bearing rose. *HortScience* 41: 1013.

Kováts, E. 1987. Composition of essential oils. Part 7. Bulgarian oil of rose (*Rosa damascena Mill.*). *J. Chromatogr.* 406: 185-222.

Krüssmann, G. 1981. *The Complete Book of Roses.* Portland, Oregon: Timber Press.

Kurkcuoglu, M., and K. H. C. Baser. 2003. Studies on Turkish rose concrete, absolute, and hydrosol. *Chem. Nat. Compd.* 39: 457-464.

Kwaselow, A., et al. 1990. Rose hips: A new occupational allergen. *J. Allergy Clin. Immunol.* 85: 704-708.

Lawrence, B. M. 1991. *Progress in essential oils. Perfumer Flavor.* 16(3): 43-44, 46, 51-52, 54-56, 58-64, 66-70, 72-74, 76-77.

Loghmani-Khouzani, H., et al. 2007. Essential oil composition of *Rosa damascena* Mill cultivated in central Iran. *Sci. Iran.* 14: 316-319.

MacGregor, J. C. 1980. *A Portfolio of Rose Hips.* Palo Alto, California: Sweetbriar Press.

McGimpsey, J. A. 1993. *Rose–Rosa damascena* 'Trigintipetala.' New Zealand Inst. Crop Food Res. Broadsheet No. 29.

Moore, R. S. 1963. Mist propagation of miniature roses. *Proc. Int. Pl. Propag.* Soc. 13: 208-210.

Naqvi, A. A., and S. Mandel. 1997. Investigation of rose oils from different places in India by capillary gas chromatography. *J. Med. Aromatic Pl. Sci.* 19: 1000-1002.

Nowak, R. 2004. Chemical composition of hips essential oil of some *Rosa* L. species. Z. *Naturforsch.* 60c: 369-378.

Oka, N., et al. 1999. Aroma evolution during flower opening in *Rosa damascena* Mill. Z. *Naturforsch.* 54c: 889-895.

Palairet, M. 1999. Primary production in a market for luxury: the rose-oil trade of Bulgaria, 1771-1941. *J. Eur. Econ. Hist.* 28: 551-597.

Phillips, R., and M. Rix. 1988. *Roses.* New York: Random House.

Rusanov, K., et al. 2005. Microsatellite analysis of *Rosa damascena* Mill. accessions reveals genetic similarity between genotypes used for rose oil production and old damask rose varieties. *Theor. Appl. Genet.* 111: 804-809.

Scalliet, G., et al. 2002. Biosytnhesis of the major scent components 3,5-dimethyloxytoluene and 1,3,5-trimethoxybenzene by novel rose O-methyltransferases. *FEBS Lett.* 523:113-118.

_____, et al. 2006. Role of petal-specific orcinal O-methyltransferases in the evolution of rose scent. *Pl. Physiol.* 140: 18-29.

Schieber, A., et al. 2005. Flavonol glycosides from distilled petals of *Rosa damascena* Mill. Z. *Naturforsch.* 60c: 379-384.

Singh, S. P., et al. 2000. Correlated response for increased flower yield in 'damask rose' (*Rosa damascena* Mill). *Sci. Lett.* 23(7/8): 95-97.

Stock, K. L. 1984. *Rose Books.* Milton Keynes, England: K. Stock.

Thomas, G. S. 1979. *The Old Shrub Roses.* Rev. ed. London: J. M. Dent & Sons.

Tucker, A. O., and M. J. Maciarello. 1986. Nomenclature and chemistry of the Kazanlik damask rose and some potential alternatives from the horticultural trade of North America and Europe. In *Flavor and Fragrances: A World Perspective.* Ed. B. M. Lawrence et al. Amsterdam: Elsevier. 99-114.

Umezu, T., et al. 2002. Anticonflict effects of rose oil and identification of its active constituents. *Life Sci.* 72: 91-102.

Verrier, S. 1991. *Rosa rugosa.* Deer Park, Wisconsin: Capability's Books.

Vinokur, Y., et al. 2006. Rose petal tea as an antioxidant-rich beverage: cultivar effects. *J. Food Sci.* 71: S42-S47.

Wissemann, V., and C. M. Ritz. 2005. The genus *Rosa* (Rosoideae, Rosaceae) revisited: molecular analysis of nrITS-1 and atpB-rbcL intergeneric spacer (IGS) versus conventional taxonomy. *Bot. J. Linn. Soc.* 147: 275-290.

This pass-along rose blooms from July to October
in Jeanne Calkin's garden.

Dr. Arthur O. Tucker is Research Professor and Co-Director of the Claude E. Phillips Herbarium at Delaware State University in Dover, Delaware. He is the author of numerous scientific and popular publications, including The Encyclopedia of Herbs (Timber Press, 2009). He has been a member of IHA since its inception. He is gradually re-inventing himself as a "ferro-concrete artist."

Growing Roses Sustainably

Holly H. Shimizu

AT THE U.S. Botanic Garden we have been refining the art and science of growing healthy roses organically – this was thought to be an oxymoron but we have shown that it is possible. Following is a summary of our current practices.

A sustainable approach to rose growing is important for the health of the environment as well as for pollinators. Selecting roses with lower susceptibilities, together with great horticultural practices, yields healthy roses without the application of fungicides and insecticides. This is done by promoting vigorous growth and a strong natural disease resistance. The first step is to know the basic needs for growing roses:

- At least 6 hours of direct sunlight
- Minimal root competition from nearby trees
- A soil pH of approximately 6.5
- Good air circulation
- Rose roots grow deep (2 to 3 feet) and prefer a deeply dug soil with ample organic matter

Although many great roses can be found in old cemeteries and abandoned sites and then selected for gardens, giving added attention to roses can help them look their best. Hardiness varies greatly with type, and frost protection is a must for roses whose cold tolerance is marginal for your area. It is best to grow roses on their own roots. If the plants are grafted, keep the bud union (the place where canes join the rootstock) just above the soil level. Plant bare-root roses in late winter while the plants are still dormant. Potted roses can go in the ground in spring or fall but need shelter from extreme weather.

Here are recommendations for initial planting of healthy roses:

- First, have the soil tested for an analysis of current nutrient levels, pH, etc. Typically nutrient levels will reveal a need for additional nitrogen, phosphorous and/or potassium...if so try the following organic sources:
- Kelp (1 tablespoon per plant)
- Chicken manure – broadcast a small amount
- Cotton seed meal (1 tablespoon per plant)
- Alfalfa meal (1 tablespoon per plant)
- Cocoa hulls (a handful)
- We actually mix these in a large container in these proportions and add the mix to the soil at planting time.
- Apply Epsom salts (1/4 cup per plant) if testing shows low magnesium content
- Mulch with cocoa hulls (a by-product of the chocolate industry, be careful as these can be poisonous to dogs)
- In winter, scratch in a top dressing of the nutrient mixture used at initial planting.

Periodic Fertilization

To nourish beneficial soil organisms, strengthen disease resistance, and combat the stresses of heat, urban pollution, pests and diseases, fertilization should be done every 4 to 6 weeks during the growing season, stopping in late summer.

- Plant growth activator that contain beneficial soil bacteria
- Seaweed organic fertilizer which contains kelp, vitamins, chelated micronutrients, fungi and humic acid
- Remove aphids with a hard spray of cold water

Rose Pruning

First determine if the rose blooms on old or on new wood. Roses that bloom on old wood include many of the species roses and the old European roses. These are pruned more lightly in late winter. Roses such as teas, chinas, and some new shrub roses, bloom on new growth and can therefore tolerate a harder prune.

When roses are first planted they require minimal pruning. Once established, try to keep three different years of growth – current, 1-year old, 2-year old branches.

- Prune all dead, diseased, crossing and weak branches first and then step back to see what remains
- Use high quality tools, especially pruning shears and wear thick gloves
- The best time to prune is in late winter just when the buds are beginning to swell, but at least one month prior to the last frost
- Cut on an angle, just above the buds which face the direction of desired growth (usually away from the plant). Do the same when deadheading.

Based on the U.S. Botanic Garden's evaluations here are the recommendations (remember that each year and each location can have varying results!):

- **'Betty Prior'** – great bloomer, single pink, very minor black spot
- **'Blanc Double de Coubert'** – low, open habit, fragrant, coarse foliage
- **'Carefree Beauty'** – large, loose, semi-double pink, light fragrance, Minor black spot
- **'Graham Thomas'** – a solid performer, good fragrance, interesting butterscotch color
- **'Heritage'** – always nice, pink, double, very fragrant
- **'Louise Odier'** – wonderful fragrance, old-fashioned double pink
- **'Marie Pavie'** – a nice small plant with gorgeous, fragrant flowers
- **'Mrs. Dudley Cross'** – nice blend, loosely double, good rebloom
- **'Pat Austin'** – great warm color, a good performer

- **'Pretty Lady'** – small shrub, cream to creamy pink flowers
- ***R. chinensis* v. *mutabilis*** – lovely, everblooming shrub or climber in warmer areas
- **'Roseraie de l'Hay'** – magenta flowers, fragrant, thorny, informal habit of rugosa roses
- **'Spice'** – a small plant, double pink flowers
- **'The Pilgrim'** – pale yellow, double flowers, good repeat bloom

This information has been gathered by a host of gardeners and our Curator over the years of growing roses organically and evaluating them yearly at the U.S. Botanic Garden.

Holly H. Shimizu is the Executive Director of the U.S. Botanic Garden located on the Mall in Washington, DC. They grow roses organically and focus on sustainable gardening in their gardens, education, and outreach programs. In addition to being the first Curator of the National Herb Garden from 1980 to 1988 Holly has traveled and widely continues with her passionate interest in herbs. Holly lives in Glen Echo, Maryland with her husband Osamu, a garden designer, and her naughty dog, Fuji. She spends much of her free time working in their sanctuary garden.

The Queen of Flowers

Pat Crocker

"Whereas there has long represented love, friendship, peace and the devotion of the American people to their country… that the flower commonly known as the rose is designated and adopted as the national floral emblem of the United States of America." ….

---Joint Resolution of the Senate and House of the 99th Congress

ACTING ON THE above resolution in 1986, President Ronald Reagan declared the noble rose to be the National Flower of the United States of America. And since proof abounds that the rose has graced American soil longer than any human, a better choice could not have been made. Indeed, rose imprints on slate deposits in the Florissant Fossil Beds near Cripple Creek, Colorado have been identified as being around 35 to 40 million years old—a lineage old enough to warrant that this stately blossom be crowned queen of the land.

The roses that were blooming near Cripple Creek during the Oligocene epoch were 'wild species' roses that probably originated in Central Asia. They were hardy, with simple single flowers growing on shrubs or climbing cane-like shoots. Their rose hips were almost as big as the flower itself. Wild Species roses are the plants from which all modern roses descend. *Rosa rugosa* is the best modern-day example of wild species roses (see Rose Classification).

It is believed that some 5,000 years ago, the Chinese began cultivating the rose (Oriental species roses had one advantage over the European/Mediterranean group of species: they were *remontant*, or repeat bloomers). Throughout antiquity the rose was associated with the simple pleasures of life, with myths and legends, and with the rituals and ceremonies of religions. Egyptian tombs have revealed wreaths of Damask-like roses dating to about AD 170, Minoan frescoes (c. 1700 BC) in Crete at Knossos feature roses in their design, and the Romans developed the first hot houses in order to feed their voracious appetite for the floral monarch. It was the Roman goddess Venus whose amorous indiscretions prompted Cupid to bribe the God of Silence with a rose making it the symbol for secrecy. The term 'sub rosa', which has survived from Roman times (when ceilings were decorated with roses to remind diners to guard the secrecy of dinner conversations), to this day means confidentially.

The focus on religion and herbal medicine during the Middle Ages defined the use of the rose for medicinal purposes. Monks developed and perfected distillation techniques and were using roses for eye ointments and salves, syrups, powders, oils, conserves, scented rosary beads, candied condiments and in baked products. Crusaders, gypsies, artists and artisans were spreading the reign of the rose from the Middle East, northern Africa and Eastern Europe.

Royal connections to the rose were strengthened in the 15th century during England's War of the Roses. The House of York adopted a white rose (possibly *R. alba*) and the House of Lancaster took a red rose (possibly *R. gallica*) as its emblem. After 30 years of civil war, Henry VII emerged victorious, married a York princess, and united the families in a new Tudor dynasty. He merged his Lancastrian rose with the white rose of his York bride and thus created the Tudor Rose, the Rose of England.

The 19th century marked a dividing point between 'old' roses and 'modern' roses. The Dutch began systematically growing roses from seed and in the early part of the 1800s introduced the first hybrid roses, among them, the Centifolia varieties. The French painter, Pierre-Joseph Redoute immortalized the rose in his paintings for Empress Josephine who also encouraged the hybridizing of new roses. Working mostly with *Gallica*, *Damask*, *Alba* and *Centifolia* roses, French breeders Dupont and Descemet developed several hundred new cultivars using controlled cross-breeding techniques. Around this time, the highly prized continuous-blooming roses were introduced to Europe from China and India. The Oriental roses arrived by ship along with another precious cargo, that of tea—from which the term 'Tea rose' derives. But the eastern roses were far too tender to survive the temperate European climate and were cross-bred with winter-hardy varieties and in 1867, the first 'Hybrid Tea' roses were introduced.

In 1972, an English garden consultant by the name of Graham Stuart Thomas planned and laid out the rose garden at Mottisfont Abbey in Hampshire, England. The abbey itself dates back to the second century when William the Conquer owned it. Its name is derived from the font or spring that can still be found on the property. Mottisfont was an Augustinian priory right up until the Dissolution when it slipped into private residence around the mid-1700s. The last private owner transferred Mottisfont to the National Trust in 1957.

The rose garden at Mottisfont Abbey is remarkable due to Thomas' foresight in planting pre-1900 roses. The collection has now been registered as 'The National Collection of Shrub Roses prior to 1900' by the National Council for the Conservation of Plants and Gardens in England. I had the privilege of visiting Mottisfont's rose garden, at its best in midsummer. It is spectacular. With provision for some 300 varieties, it has a good selection of species roses from different parts of the world and a generous representation of the early 19th century French hybrids. The coloring, style and fragrance of these roses have never been surpassed and they are displayed brilliantly at Mottisfont.

Surrounded by high red-brick walls that once contained the abbey's kitchen garden, the garden's four large quadrants are defined by two main lavender-lined paths. The central focus is a circle of arches exploding with alternating light pink ('Debutante') and dark ('Bleu Magenta') blue-magenta blossoms. Under-plantings of herbs and perennial flowers give the garden depth and character while extending the color throughout the season.

Standing in the very center of the rose-draped arbors at Mottisfont Abbey, one absorbs the history of the majestic rose almost as one inhales the fragrant perfume, and begins to grasp the tremendous reign of power this old-as-time plant has wielded.

Classifying Roses

CLASSIFICATION OF ROSES can be daunting, even to the passionate rose gardener. Roses belong to the third largest plant family, the Rosaceae Family. Plants in this group are characterized by five petals and the shape of the hip, and include hawthorn (*Crataegus laevigata*), meadowsweet (*Filipendula ulmaria*), creeping cinquefoil (*Potentilla reptans*), plums and cherries (*Prunus* genus), salad burnet (*Sanguisorba minor*), along with apples, pears wild strawberries and raspberries.

The genus name of roses is *Rosa*. Roses can be found on bushes or on long canes known as climbers. They may bloom only once in a season or continually throughout; they may be brilliantly perfumed or virtually non-odiferous; the number of petals ranges from five to hundreds; and their color ranges from white to orange to red and purple and every shade in-between. Those physical attributes are now being used by landscapers and nurseries as a way to group roses (because they pinpoint the purpose to which roses may be used in gardens). However, there is an older, more established system of classifying roses that places them into three basic categories—Wild Species Roses, Old Garden Roses and Modern Roses.

Species Roses (wild)

ONE TO TWO hundred (some say there are around 120 true species roses and about the same number that are classified as species but are generally garden forms or hybrids) wild rose species exist today. Species roses are truly the first flowers still in existence with the following characteristics:

- Thought to have evolved perhaps as long ago as 60 million years and spread from central Asia to all parts of the Northern Hemisphere (North America, Europe and Asia)
- Genetically pure strains from which all roses descend

- Tough, disease-resistant; some are cold-hardy; many thrive on impoverished soil; most have large fleshy hips; most bear small flowers with five petals in a single layer—called a 'single'; most bloom only once (China and Tea roses being the exception as repeat bloomers)
- Good for herb, wild or naturalistic gardens or shrub borders
- May be climbing (rambler or climber) or non-climbing (shrub)

Gertrude Jekyll was a great fan of species roses. Her 1920 book, *Roses for English Gardens* describes 38 species roses. A dozen species rose varieties are listed below (note that some of them also fall into the Old Garden Roses class; dates in brackets are discovery dates):

- **R. blanda** - North American native (1773); large pink flowers; also called Hudson's Bay or Labrador Rose.
- **R. canina** – British native (1737); known as Dog Rose; hips high in vitamin C.
- **R. centifolia** – the type of the Cabbage or Provence Roses
- **R. damascena** (Damask)—from Damascus is a hybrid between—R. *gallica* and R. *phoenicea*; several varieties, red, white and striped. It is now used in Bulgaria for the extraction of rose water and attar for the perfume industry.
- **R. eglantaria** – European native (1551) grows up to 10 feet, single pink flowers, apple-scented foliage; known as Sweetbrier.
- **R. gallica** – France to Persia native (1310); deep pink, medium- sized, semi-double flowers; the type of most of the older garden roses. It was thought to be a religious emblem of the Medes and Persians in the 12th century BC. *Gallica officinalis* was brought from Damascus by the Crusaders and spawned the medicinal rose industry in the medieval town of Provins, France, thus called 'Apothecary' Rose. A striped red and white sport* appeared during or before the 16th century and

was dubbed 'Rosa Mundi'. *Gallica* and *damascena* are the forbears to the modern Hybrid Perpetuals.

- **R. glauca** – European native (1830); tiny 1-inch, bright-pink single flowers, gray/purple foliage turns red in autumn.
- **R. lucida** – North American native; large bushes, rose-colored flowers.
- **R. multiflora** – Eastern Asia native (1810); large bushes; the parent of many rambling roses.
- **R. rugosa** – far north Pacific Rim regions native; extremely hardy with showy hips; 'Hansa' and 'Rose a Parfum de l'Hay' are two purple varieties.
- **R. virginiana** – North American (1640); single, large medium- pink flower on upright and bushy growth with light-green, glossy leaves; good scent.
- **R. wichuriana** – Japanese native (1891); trailing with small leaves and white flowers.

*sport – a spontaneous mutation that generates a new rose.

Old Garden Roses

THE AMERICAN ROSE Society defines Old Garden Roses as those types that existed before 1867, the year the first Hybrid Tea was introduced. Here are a few of the hundreds of Old Garden Roses in existence today:

Non-climbing

- **R. alba** –it is generally believed that the alba 'Semiplena' was the 'White Rose of York'; large branching shrubs with
- Clusters of white, cream, blush or pink flowers on upright plants; 'Maidens Blush' and 'Celeste' are popular varieties.
- **'Bourbon'** – *R. damascena bifera* crossed with hybrid China roses on the Isle de Bourbon in the Indian Ocean; vigorous, open, repeat-flowering shrubs with fragrant double flowers.

- **R centifolia** (Cabbage or Provence) – Dutch hybridized; excellent sweet-smelling, double flowers (*centifolia* means literally, 100 petals). It has been used on cretonne and wallpaper, thus is known as 'Rose des Peintres' (rose of the painters).
- **'China'** (*R. chinensis*) - small to medium shrub roses with small, mostly double flowers, single or in clusters; spicy fragrance.
- **'Damask'** (*R. damascena*) – fragrant blooms in clusters of 5 to 7 grow on loose, large shrubs; examples: 'Madame Hardy' (white) and 'Omar Kayyam' (lilac).
- **'Gallica'** (Apothecary) – see above; once-blooming brilliant, dense and shrubby, disease-free fragrant roses; examples: 'Agatha' (pale pink) and 'Constance Spry' (pink).
- **'Hybrid Perpetual'** – *R. damascena bifera* crossed with hybrid China roses; pink and red flowers, often re-blooming; vigorous tall shrubs.
- **'Hybrid Sweet Briar'** – see *eglantaria* above.
- **'Moss'** – a 'sport'* of *R. centifolia* that appeared in the late 17th century; named for the velvety growth on stems and calyx; many-petaled blooms; generally winter-hardy.
- **'Portand'** - usually re-blooming, fragrant, double flowers; upright dense bushes.
- **'Scotch'**- (*pimpinellifolia*).
- **'Tea'** (*R. odorata gigantea*) – Bourbon Roses crossed with hybrid China roses; re-blooming sweetly-scented double flowers.

Climbing

- **'Boursault'**
- **'Climbing Tea'**
- **'Climbing Bourbon'**
- **'Noisette'** – re-blooming, graceful climbers (up to 20 feet) with large clusters of small fragrant flowers.

- **'Rambler'** – usually have many smaller, once-blooming flowers in large bunches; rapid growers, ideal for covering large areas.

Modern Roses

ALL MODERN ROSES can trace their geneology right back to a few—some say only 10—species roses. Hybridizers develop new varieties using time-tested methods of cross-breeding.

Bush

- **Floribunda** – compact (2 feet), adaptable; produce quantities of flowers in clusters; one of the best types of roses for landscaping
- **Grandiflora** - Introduced in 1955, the hybrid 'Queen Elizabeth' created a new category of Modern Roses. Bigger (to 8 feet) and hardier than Hybrid Teas, they bear single or clustered flowers on long stems.
- **Hybrid Tea** – beautiful long-stemmed flowers ideal for cutting; this has been the most popular type of rose bush.
- **Polyantha** – small compact re-bloomers with small delicate flowers in large sprays.

Shrub

SHRUB ROSES ARE tough and have a prolific bloom. They are excellent choices for hedges and landscape plantings.

- **English Rose** – David Austin of England introduced his hybrids in the 1960s and created a new category of rose. English roses are a combination of Old Garden Roses offering beauty of form, color and fragrance, and repeat-blooming, disease-resistant Modern Roses.
- **Hybrid Musk**
- **Hybrid Rugosa**

ᴥᵍ **Unclassified Modern Shrub**

Climber

ᴥᵍ **Large-flowered**
ᴥᵍ **Cluster-flowered**

Miniature

MINIATURE ROSES ARE tiny replicas (6 to 30 inches) of full-size rose plants; small, abundant flowers; ideal for small spaces, containers, edging plants.

ᴥᵍ **Miniature Climbing**
ᴥᵍ **Miniature Micro-miniature**

Mini-Flora

ROSES THAT FALL between Miniature and Floribunda in size.

Ground Cover

TRAILING OR SPREADING low-growers, mostly re-bloomers with small leaves and flowers that cluster.

Sources

Associations

The American Rose Society—founded in 1899, with now over 20,000 members in local affiliates throughout the United States. P.O. Box 30,000, Shreveport, Louisiana, 71130-0030, (318) 938-5402, www.ars.org.

The Canadian Rose Society—a valuable resource on growing and knowing roses, with a Canadian viewpoint. The Canadian Rose Society c/o Barb Munton, Membership Secretary, #100 Chancellor Avenue, Victoria, British Columbia, Canada, V8Z 1R4. http://www.canadianrosesociety.org/

The Heritage Rose Foundation—a nonprofit organization devoted to the preservation of old garden roses. P.O. Box 831414, Richardson, Texas, 75083, www.heritagerosefoundation.org/.

The Royal National Rose Society—a gardening charity dedicated to encouraging, improving and extending the science, art and practice of the cultivation and conservation of roses. Chiswell Green, St. Albans, Hertfordshire, Great Britain, AL2 3NR, England. www.rnrs.org.

Books

Griffiths, Trevor. *The Book of Classic Old Roses.* New York, New York: Penguin Books, 1986.

Austin, David, *The English Roses.* Richmond Hill, Ontario, Canada: Firefly Books, 2007.

Reddell, Rayford Clayton, *The Rose Bible.* New York, New York: Harmony Books, 1994.

Schneider, Peter, *Right Rose Right Place.* North Adams, Massachusetts: Storey Publishing, 2009.

Walheim, Lance, *Roses for Dummies.* Foster City, California: IDG Books, 1997. An excellent reference for gardens, nurseries and equipment.

Web Sites

www.amityheritageroses.com-mail order roses from Hydesville, California.

www.rosarian.com-a site devoted to roses; includes a reprint of Gertrude Jekyll's 1902 classic, Roses for English Gardens.

www.oldrosenursery.com-good site for information; mail order plants in Canada only.

www.rosefile.com-good site for information.

www.rose-roses.com-good photographs of many varieties.

Nurseries

The following is a short list of nurseries specializing in old garden roses:

Antique Rose Emporium – display gardens in Brenham and San Antonio; wholesale (Texas only); their Guide to Antique Roses is an excellent handbook. 9300 Lueckemeyer Road, Brenham, Texas, 77833; 800-441-0002, www.antiqueroseemporium.com.

Heirloom Roses – an online mail order resource for old garden roses. 24062 NE Riverside Drive, Saint Paul, Oregon, 97137; 503-538-1576, www.heirloomroses.com

High Country Roses – a good selection of hardy roses including antique, shrub and species roses. PO Box 148, Jensen, Utah, 84053; 800-552-2082, www.highcountryroses.com

Petals From the Past – excellent source of old garden plants and some new varieties and an excellent resource for southern gardeners. Located south of Birmingham, Alabama; 205-646-0069, www.petalsfromthepast.com

Rose Gardens

Antique Rose Emporium – see full listing under Nurseries

Boone Hall Plantation – antique roses that are over 100 years old still growing at the site. 1235 Long Point Road, Mount Pleasant, South Carolina, 29464; 843-884-4371,www.boonehallplantation.com

Elizabeth Park – Oldest municipally operated rose garden in the United States with 2.5 acres and about 15,000 rose bushes. P.O. Box 370361, West Hartford, Connecticut, 06137-0361; 860-242-0017, www.elizabethpark.org

Gladney Rose Garden – The Missouri Botanical Garden, 4344 Shaw Blvd., St. Louis, Missouri, 63110; 800-642-8842, www.mobot.org

Heirloom Roses – see full listing under Nurseries

Huntington Botanical Gardens – 1151 Oxford Rd., San Marino, California, 91108; 626-405-2140, www.huntington.org

International Rose Test Garden – Washington Park, 400 S.W. Kingston Ave., Portland, Oregon, 97201; 503-823-7529, www.portlandonline.com/parks/finder

Peggy Rockefeller Rose Garden – displays 4,000 plants, over 600 varieties. The NY Botanical Garden, 2900 Southern Blvd., Bronx, New York, 10458-5126; 718-817-8616, www.nybg.org

"Gather Ye Roses While Ye May... "

---Robert Louis Stevenson

*Pat Crocker is a writer, photographer, author of thirteen cookbooks (including 3 herb handbooks and her latest book, **Preserving**); she is passionate about food and herbs. She loves her work as a culinary herbalist and is always on the hunt for a new rose or rose garden to photograph. Pat is the humble recipient of both the Gertrude Foster Book Award (HSA, 2009) and the 2011 IHA Professional Award. Her books have won international awards, most notably, Best in the World (for her book, **The Vegan Cook's Bible**) from the International Gourmand Culinary Awards.*

Antique Rose Care Guide
Antique Rose Emporium

Preparing a Rose Bed

"ANTIQUE ROSES" ARE hardy even in poor conditions, but they will be at their best if planted in a favorable situation with rich, well-drained soil. The best place to plant a rose is in an open area that receives at least six hours of direct sunlight daily and allows air movement around each plant.

Good soil preparation will make a great difference in the health and long-term vigor of your roses. The best place to start is to have your soil tested for nutrient content and pH. The ideal pH for roses is around 6.5, but roses will tolerate soils that are slightly alkaline or slightly more acidic. Contact your local county extension agent for information on soil testing.

Incorporating organic matter such as composted manure, composted bark, or a good landscaping soil amendment into the soil of your bed before planting will both enrich a sandy soil and break up a heavy clay soil to allow for proper drainage. Adding coarse sand in addition to the organic matter will also help to loosen heavy soils. As the organic matter continues to decompose, it will add nutrients to the soil, help promote the activity of beneficial soil micro-organisms, and will help neutralize soil pH. (We don't recommend using peat moss, peat-based soil amendments, or large volumes of mushroom compost because they have not given satisfactory results.)

Planting the Roses

Dig the hole large enough to accommodate the root ball. The plant should be set approximately the same level at which it was growing in its pot. Add enough soil to cover the roots, then firm well and water thoroughly to remove air pockets and to settle the soil firmly around the root system. Fill the rest of the hole with soil and mound it slightly around the base of the plant for stability while settling.

Potted roses can also be transplanted into large containers and grown indefinitely in this manner until you choose a permanent location. Remember to use a high quality potting soil when transplanting from one pot to another. Roses grown in containers require water and fertilizer more frequently than those planted in the ground, and have the same sunlight requirement of at least six hours.

Mulching and Watering

A thick layer of mulch applied 1 or 2 times a year means fewer weeds, less water stress, less heat stress, richer soil, and healthier plants. We use a native mulch on our beds, but leaf mulch or any weed-free material will do the job.

Rose varieties that have survived for years are usually drought tolerant once established (about 2 years), but your plants will look much better if they get a good, deep soaking every 5 to 7 days when conditions are dry, including winter. This is better than a frequent light sprinkling which only encourages the roots to grow near the surface where they are vulnerable to stress and damage. Deep watering will encourage your roses to hold their foliage and bloom better in the summer months. A soaker hose or some form of drip irrigation, run for several hours at a time, works especially well to minimize water waste through evaporation and to keep the rose leaves dry. Another method of deep watering would be to leave your garden hose trickling slowly until the ground is saturated.

Feeding

We have found that most slow-release, commercial rose foods and organic fertilizers are fine and give good results if directions are followed carefully. Have your soil tested to determine your specific needs.

The important thing about any fertilizer application is that it should be watered in thoroughly after application; both to dissolve the fertilizer into a form the rose can use and to clean any residue off the surrounding foliage. Chemical fertilizers can burn or even kill a plant if over-used or improperly applied. Read the label and when in doubt about how much to apply, remember that less is better, and always water well afterward. (We do not recommend using fertilizers that contain any herbicides, systemic insecticides, or systemic fungicides because these products have been known to damage or kill plants.)

For those who simply want to keep their roses healthy and blooming well, a feeding in spring and another in late summer should suffice. It is also advisable to stop fertilizing at least six weeks before your first frost date. This will help your plants to slow their growth in order to go dormant for winter and avoid freeze damage.

Disease and Insects

If your old roses seem to be unduly affected by blackspot or powdery mildew, they are most likely planted in the wrong spot: too much shade, too little air circulation, poorly drained soil, etcetera. An old rose properly situated should give years of basically trouble-free beauty. This is not to say that the "Antique Roses" never get blackspot or mildew. They are disease resistant, but rarely disease free. They will generally shed any infected leaves, continuing to grow and bloom with healthy vigor. If you choose to spray in order to keep the foliage perfect, we suggest on an "as needed" basis rather than a regular preventative program.

Aphids, thrips, and other insect pests rarely affect a healthy rose severely, but they can disfigure and damage the tender new growth, buds, and flowers. We suggest using insecticidal soap for the control of most insect pests on roses since it is environmentally safe, it is very safe for the person spraying, and because insects cannot build up a resistance to it. Spider mites can be controlled by a vigorous hosing of the leaves with water and by thoroughly spraying both surfaces of the leaves afterwards with insecticidal soap or liquid seaweed.

We suggest using strong chemical insecticides only in the case of very severe infestations which might result in the loss of the plant. An organic approach is preferred.

Pruning

"Antique Roses" don't require the stringent and careful pruning that is needed by many modern sorts. A good rule of thumb is to clip back no more than one-third of the bush, encouraging full foliage and heavy bloom without destroying the vigor and natural attractive form of the plant.

When a rose bush, like any other shrub, is cut back, it responds by putting on a spurt of growth. This tender new growth can get frost or heat-burned, so avoid heavy midsummer or late fall pruning, or pruning too early in the spring. Two to three weeks before the final frost date is ideal for spring pruning.

Ever-blooming varieties can be lightly trimmed or "tip-pruned" several times a year, as they flower on new growth. Roses that bloom but once are best pruned after they have bloomed. Their flowers come from wood that has hardened over a winter, so early spring pruning will reduce their floral display.

Our pruning regimen involves cutting back about one-third of each rose bush (some more and some less) each spring, sometime around Valentine's Day (February 14). Unbalanced growth is removed and any dead canes and twigs are also removed, which makes for a healthier plant. We continue to prune and deadhead throughout the summer. In late summer (September in our area), we give the bushes a light, overall haircut to encourage the repeat-flowering roses to flush out beautifully in the fall and to give the spring bloomers a tidier shape.

Climbing roses really need only to have any dead or unwanted canes removed and to have their canes trained. Sometimes it is advantageous to remove old canes thoroughly in order to make room for newer, more productive ones. If a climber is getting too big and bushy it is best to thin it out in early spring so that you can see what you're doing while its foliage is not a bother. Spring-blooming climbers, on the other hand, should be pruned only after they have bloomed or you will risk losing all or most of their blooms.

We normally train all of our climbers thoroughly early in the spring and thin repeat bloomers if necessary. They are tidied up occasionally through the late spring and summer and then we again train them and remove any unwanted growth late in the summer. In the early summer after the spring-bloomers have finished, we remove many of their older canes to make room for the new. Sometimes it is necessary to cut the whole plant down to almost nothing in the case of some of the more vigorous ramblers.

Rose hedges can be shaped easily with hedge shears, and roses in a natural or wild setting can be left completely alone, unless a hard winter produces some unsightly dead canes. If left unpruned, many varieties of old roses will produce attractive hips to brighten the winter garden.

The Antique Rose Emporium is renowned worldwide for their quality and selection of antique roses. If you are ever in the area—you must visit—since it is an intoxicating experience. Otherwise go to the Web site to shop and/or order their catalog, which is well worth the cost. www.weAREroses.com; *for mail orders 800-441-0002.*

San Antonio Gardens, 7561 East Evans Road, San Antonio, Texas 78266 210-651-4565

Independence Gardens, 10,000 FM 50, Brenham, Texas 77833 979-836-5548

Rose Lady

History & Lore

Climbing roses should be supported by trellises; this trellis at the Antique
Rose Emporium features a different cultivar on each section.

Roses:
A Northern Perspective

Carol Little

ROSES ARE ALIVE and well in Canada. This is a fun fact that surprises many of my friends around the world, who, mistakenly think of my homeland as the land of 'everlasting winter'. It is true that most of Canada's 33 million people reside in the southern part of the country, and that, regardless of our location; most would agree that our winters are too long. That being said, we are avid rose enthusiasts, from coast to coast. The rose family (Rosaceae) is very large and many are surprised to learn that it includes apple, apricot, crabapple, hawthorn, peach, pear, raspberry, strawberry and serviceberry.

Canada's short growing season and blustery cold winters have prompted the development of roses that can withstand these harsh conditions. In the 1800s, Canadians, fascinated with roses and the challenge of our climate, were inspired to create the first "Canadian hybrids".

In 1886, the Canadian government began a program to do just that by establishing a number of experimental farms. This program produced many winter-hardy lilies, lilacs and some delightful shrub roses. In 1946, it was temporarily suspended due to the retirement of the director, Isabella Preston.

Also in the 1940s, researchers in Morden, Manitoba developed a series renowned for exceptional blooms from native prairie roses. More recently, the Morden research station has created "the Parkland series"; gorgeous blooms, able to withstand long, dry winters and unpredictable springs. Parkland roses are very disease-resistant (notably resistant to blackspot fungus).

In the 1960s, the Central Experimental Farm resumed operation, in the nation's capitol, Ottawa, and researchers under Dr. Svejda created "the Explorer series". Researchers produced modern shrub roses; a combination of hardy roses and tea roses which were bred for the tough humid climate of Eastern Canada. These need very little pruning, are hardy to zones 2 and 3, and are resistant to insects, disease and mildew. The series pays homage to the great European explorers who, themselves, survived many a harsh winter! I've been told that there are over 20 Explorer roses on the market, today, which will bloom across the entire country, needing very little maintenance with the exception of a solid snow cover during winter months.

In 1998, the *Canadian Artists Rose Consortium* was formed after the government rose-breeding program closed. At the time, apparently, there were more than 15,000 rose cells in the plant vaults in Ottawa. This exciting new group of Canadian rose growers and breeders has released two varieties, in 2007, named after Canadian artists: Emily Carr and Felix Leclerc. These new roses are a marriage of some of the best of the original work from Ottawa and the devoted participation of rose-breeders from across Canada. This new series will be able to be grown in every part of the country in zones 2 to 6 and promises to be the toughest, yet most refined to-date!

The Canadian hybrids are now world renowned, offering the northern gardener a chance to enjoy glorious fragrant plants able to over-winter in any climate! There are many Rose Societies and well-loved Rose gardens in Canada. I can't list them all here but must include two of my favourites. See reference information at the end of this chapter.

A comment about Rose gardens would not be complete without mentioning the famed Butchart Gardens; 55 acres close to Victoria on Vancouver Island on the west coast. The usually mild climate in the greater Vancouver area normally provides ideal growing conditions for any and all roses. In the winter of 2011, an unusually harsh winter destroyed over 1,200 roses—so visitors will now have the chance to enjoy an extraordinary new rose garden, courtesy of Mother Nature and much hard work on the part of the team of gardeners!

The Royal Botanical Gardens, Canada's largest botanical gardens, features both cultivated and wild gardens. Located near Toronto in Burlington, Ontario, this huge teaching garden is always fun to visit, with activities of interest to young and old. The Rose Festival takes place each June and is well attended by rose enthusiasts who are treated to a truly spectacular show.

My personal affection for roses goes back to my childhood, in my parents' garden and a special rose called the 'Roundelay'. I can still recall the intoxicating scent of this deep crimson, avid bloomer, who for me was always the star of that early garden.

Our tiny urban garden, these days, is packed with roses of all colours and yes, one of the Canadian Explorers; 'William Baffin' and a Parkland, 'Morden Ruby'. We are fortunate to have a very abundant blooming *Rosa rugosa*, as well, which shares its petals and rose hips with us each year.

I confess to simply enjoying the beauty, the proud display of blooms, the sweet aromas wafting through our garden, and I find it shocking that I have lost track of some of their names! However I love them all and find such joy here and am captivated by each new fragrant gift. Carol shares the enchanting aroma of the rose further on in *Recipes: The Apothecary*.

Sources

Canadian Artists Roses www.canadianartistsroses.com
Canadian Rose Society www.canadianrosesociety.org
Butchart Gardens www.butchartgardens.com
Royal Botanical Gardens www.rbg.ca

This vivid floribunda is aply named 'Orangeade'.

Carol Little, R.H. is a traditional herbalist in Toronto, Canada. She is a past board member and current professional member of the Ontario Herbalists Association. <u>www.herbalists.on.ca</u>

She combines her love of travel and passion for all things green and loves to write about both. Carol is a regular contributor to the International Herb Association newsletter as one of the regional reporters. When time permits, she writes a health-focused, herb-inspired blog for her clients and her community. <u>www.studiobotanica.com</u>

Rose is a Rose is a Rose—
except when it's a symbol

Gert Coleman

"But he that dares not grasp the thorn
should never crave the rose."

---Anne Bronte (English poet, novelist 1820-1849)

ROSES ARE SEXY, the sensuous symbol of love and passion. Yet roses (*Rosa* spp. Rosaceae) have become so embedded within our culture that we take them for granted, even see them as clichés at times. What would Valentine's Day or Mother's Day, for example, be without a bouquet of red roses?

Rightful stars of gardens and bouquets, roses have cultivated their places in literature, history, magic, medicine, and word usage. Roses usually symbolize beauty and love, but symbols have more than one side. Thorns, also called prickles, remind us of all the painful complications that come with passion. Falling in love does not always have a happy outcome.

Roses occur in many legends, fairy tales, poems, songs, and novels. I love stories and I love roses. While stories can entertain, they often reveal customs, traditions, morals, values, and practical applications. Roses are a thorny issue. They're hard to grow, need full-sun, get all kinds of diseases, and have thorns. People get snooty about their roses, too, lineage, growing patterns, and the like. Plant descriptions in literature can help to depict setting or function as images and metaphors to add depth to plot, character, and mood.

Ancient Mediterranean goddess of love Aphrodite has long been associated with roses. Often depicted in artwork standing on a large shell, Aphrodite was born of sea foam, with roses trailing in her wake. Folklore suggests that her bath water was the origin of rose water. Along with apples, lilies, pomegranates, and myrtle, roses were sacred to Aphrodite, later known as Venus, and roses bloomed in her temple gardens throughout the Mediterranean region.

Revered in Christianity, the Virgin Mary was honored with roses throughout medieval abbey gardens and in the rosary, whose beads were originally made from powdered roses. Her statues were often crowned with wreaths of white roses, symbolizing purity. Red and pink roses, by comparison, often signal passion and romance. According to Diana De-Luca, author of *Botanica Erotica*, the sensuous, diverse pinks and reds of rosebuds and petals have reminded many of the erotic parts of a woman's body - from facial blushes (a rosy hue) to nipples and lips. In English, *rose* is one of the words for the colors red and pink, and, in fairy tales, beautiful women are often named Rose.

DeLuca believes that rose's scent can both open hearts and heal broken ones. Rose petals have been strewn at weddings, floated in baths and cordials, threaded into wreaths and love circles. Rose water can be sprayed directly on the body or on sheets to enhance the mood or added to honey as a love syrup to be drizzled over fruits and berries (98). During the reign of Louis XVI, the French court created love potions with roses, dill, cinnamon, and fennel. In fact, it is rare to see a love potion or aphrodisiac recipe without rose petals, rose water, or rose hips.

Cleopatra (60-30 B.C.E.), known for her beauty, political acumen, and affairs with Julius Caesar and Marc Antony, often set the mood for romance with fragrance from bathing in milk with roses to scenting her sails with roses and incense to announce her arrival to the entire harbor. According to one legend, when Marc Antony visited Cleopatra on her barge, they stood knee-deep in rose petals. Upon his death, Antony asked Cleopatra to anoint his tomb with rose petals and perfume (Gordon 18).

Under the planetary rule of Venus, roses were believed to supply clues about matters of the heart. In Scottish folklore, a white rose blooming in autumn portends an early marriage for someone. Throwing rose leaves into flames could bring good luck. If a maiden had too many suitors, she could write each name on a rose leaf, focus her thoughts on true love, then cast the leaves upon the wind. The last leaf to settle upon the ground would tell her whom to marry. Insecure lovers in ancient northern European cultures sometimes carried rose hips or "love apples" as charms to keep their lovers true.

Picking roses might have portents as well: if petals fell from a red or pink rose when you plucked it from the bush, trouble was near. But if petals dropped when plucking a white rose, it signified that your protective guardian angel was praying for you. One legend indicates that placing roses on the coffin of the recently deceased would prevent them from rising again. In addition, planting rose bushes along paths could deter vampires and other undead creatures from entering your property.

In Celtic folklore, wandering, screaming spirits could be silenced by presenting them with wild roses at every new moon. The term *sub rosa* refers to keeping certain information silent. For centuries, a white rose suspended from the ceiling indicated that all things discussed would be confidential.

Poets often use roses to appeal to the senses. In his 1648 lyric poem, "To the Virgins, to make much of time," Robert Herrick (1591-1674) uses rosebuds as symbolic images to remind us to live in the moment.

> *Gather ye rosebuds while ye may,*
> *Old time is still a-flying:*
> *And this same flower that smiles to-day*
> *To-morrow will be dying.*

The tightness of rosebuds signals the promise of youth and early summer, with all the unfurling possibilities of love, romance, and fertility. Herrick urges us not to waste time in hesitation because time will quickly rob us of our youth. Rose petals falling to the ground indicate a bloom past its prime. The poet reminds us to love as fully as possible before it's too late:

> *Then be not coy, but use your time,*
> *And while ye may, go marry:*
> *For having lost but once your prime,*
> *You may forever tarry.*

But following one's heart and succumbing to youthful passion can have consequences. In the 1842 novel *The Scarlet Letter* by Nathaniel Hawthorne, rose imagery offers insight into the Puritans, particularly Hester Prynne, in this dark tale of revenge, repression, and redemption. Old Roger Chillingworth walks into Puritan Boston after two years in Indian captivity only to see his beautiful, young wife with an infant standing on the scaffold, a scarlet letter A blazing out from her drab dress. A defiant rose in bloom, she refuses to name the father, whose punishment would be dire.

The image of the prison creates the setting and invasive weeds, symbol of insidious evil, set the tone: *"Before this ugly edifice, and between it and the wheel-track of the street, was a grass-plot, much overgrown with burdock, pigweed, apple-peru, and such unsightly vegetation...."* Seeking to root out evil and "purify" society, the Puritans strictly enforce rules with harsh punishment, even as the plants flourish outside the very door of the prison.

Hawthorne gently softens the image of rampant weeds with the wild rose, symbol of beauty, warmth, and nurture, to suggest that nature has more pity for the unfortunate sinners than the grim Puritans: *"But, on one side of the portal, and rooted almost at the threshold, was a wild rose-bush, covered, in this month of June, with its delicate gems, which might be imagined to offer their fragrance and fragile beauty to the prisoner as he went in, and to the condemned criminal as he came forth to his doom, in token that the deep heart of Nature could pity and be kind to him."*

As the reader begins to wonder how the wild rose bush will ever survive, the embodiment of that rose, Hester Prynne, exits the prison with much courage and dignity to face the unforgiving townspeople. These weeds and roses subtly suggest levels of submerged emotions and human nature.

Wild roses can be prolific, colonizing everywhere, often called "promiscuous" by rose experts (Powell 7/16/11). The rose's beauty and scent have long been desired and tiny rose plants were among the first plants to be brought to the New World, carefully tended on the long voyage from Europe (Reppert 99). In *The Scarlet Letter*, wild roses may represent nature unchecked, but many of today's cultivated varieties have been grafted onto wild rose rootstock for its vigor and resistance to disease (Scott 314).

In fairy tales, roses can symbolize inner goodness and inherent worth. In "Toads and Roses," a mother with two daughters favors the older and mistreats the younger, making her do all the household tasks. Twice a day, she travels a mile and a half to the village fountain for a pitcher of water. One day, a fairy disguised as a poor old woman begs her for a drink. The kind girl rinses the pitcher and sweetly offers water from the clearest part of the fountain. Delighted, the fairy rewards the girl's good manners: "At every word you speak, there shall come out of your mouth either a flower or a jewel."

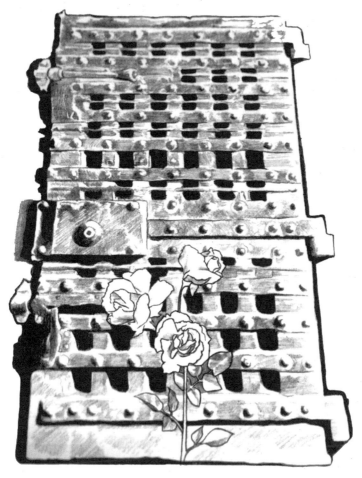

The Scarlet Letter illustration, 2008.

When her mother scolds her for being late, she apologizes and out drop two roses, two pearls, and two diamonds. The greedy mother wants the same for her favorite daughter. At the fountain, however, when the ill-tempered daughter begrudgingly gives a drink to the fairy now disguised as a well-dressed lady, the fairy curses her with vipers and toads. The mother angrily banishes the younger daughter to the forest. There she meets a prince who falls in love with her beauty and is more than satisfied with jewels and flowers as a dowry. Note that roses are as prized as diamonds and pearls. Beauty aside, roses have long been used in precious oils, perfumes, and medicine.

Stories can help us remember what plants to use for medicine. Prized for centuries for their astringent and anti-inflammatory properties, rose petals, leaves, and, in particular, rose hips have been used in Traditional Chinese Medicine (TCM) to treat diarrhea and inhibit urinary secretions.

In *Herbal Pearls: Traditional Chinese Folk Wisdom*, a collection of ancient stories passed down to illiterate peasants living through oppression and hard times to learn plant remedies, rose hips save a family's lineage. In "*Rosa laevigata, Michx.*: Jin Ying Zi," a prominent family has three sons, but two are childless. Pressured to marry and carry on the family name, the youngest son reveals an embarrassing problem: he wets the bed. Doctors are unable to help, so the family consults an old root digger who reluctantly travels to the damp, unhealthy southern region to find the necessary herb. The herbalist returns, gravely ill, with rose hips that cure the youngest son's condition but dies after handing over the medicine. The son marries and produces the much-desired heirs.

In ancient times, roses came to symbolize the excesses of the Roman Empire. At feasts and orgies, Roman emperors filled baths and fountains with rose water, made from bushels of rose petals, and seated guests on carpets of rose petals. Celebrants often wore rose garlands to prevent drunkenness. The Roman poet Horace (65-8 BC) satirically noted that excessive use of roses was starving peasants because the acreage devoted to growing roses outnumbered those of grain. During Emperor Nero's reign (54-68 AD), known for its excesses, rose petals functioned as confetti, dropped from the ceiling as guests entered celebrations.

Rose's luscious petals and enticing scent have long been associated with tactile pleasure. Today, many hybrid roses have no thorns, but that is a fairly recent development. The expression "No rose without a thorn" reminds us roses can also symbolize pain, bloodshed, and strife. The destructive English civil war, later known as the War of the Roses, lasted from 1455-1487. The war was not about roses but about lineage and throne rights. Household servants of the two warring factions wore identifying floral symbols on their livery: red for the House of Lancaster, white for the House of York. Renaissance writers, particularly William Shakespeare, linked this bloody clash to roses as factional devices. In *Henry VI, Part I*, minor lords symbolically pick sides in the rose garden:

> And here I prophesy: this brawl today,
> Grown to this faction in the Temple garden,
> Shall send, between the Red Rose and the White,
> A thousand souls to death and deadly night.

> ---Act II, Scene iv, ll. 124-8.

When Henry VII won the throne for Lancaster, the red rose became the Rose of Britain. Roses are also the national symbol of Bulgaria which leads the world in cultivation of rose oil and roses.

Roses continue to have a role in politics. After World War II, roses came to symbolize idealistic movements. In Europe and South America, labor and social activist political parties used the symbol of a red rose held in a hand to symbolize socialist and democratic ideals. During WWII, the white rose symbolized non-violent resistance groups in Germany.

Most recently, *The New York Times* printed a front page photograph of thousands of mourners carrying long-stemmed red or white roses on a "rose march" in Oslo, Norway, for a vigil in memory of the victims of an extremist terrorist attack, one of the worst mass killings in post-war Europe (*New York Times* 7/26/11).

Florists today offer a variety of colored roses for all manner of occasions. While we often choose flowers based on color preference or a color theme, roses can be ordered to suggest the subtleties of courtship and friendship. Red roses are the most popular, signifying love, passion, eternal love, and love against the odds. White roses are often used as wedding flowers and in religious ceremonies to indicate innocence and peace. Lavender roses suggest love at first sight, while deep purple roses show admiration and deep love.

Cheerful get-well bouquets feature yellow roses to suggest affection and friendship, though sometimes yellow means jealousy. Orange roses may suggest autumn colors, but orange can also be tricky. A blend of two primary colors, orange might indicate the hidden passion of red, or simply the deep affection of yellow that is not passionate love.

Roses can also have legal and economic importance. During the late Middle Ages, fines and property rents were sometimes paid in roses. According to Jean Gordon in *Pageant of the Rose*, in 1379, a minor building infraction in England could cost the violator one freshly picked rose, easily obtainable in summer, but more difficult in winter. In the 16th century, the Bishop of Ely leased his property to Queen Elizabeth's Lord Chancellor for one red rose to be paid on Midsummer Day – plus ten pounds and ten loads of hay.

Ellis Peters (1913-1995) wrote a series of herbal mysteries set during the challenging time when King Stephen and Empress Maud battled for the crown of England (1135-1150). Apothecary Brother Cadfael balances the secular daily events of Shrewsbury with the monastic obligations of a Benedictine abbey.

In *The Rose Rent*, the thirteenth chronicle of the series, a cold spring has delayed crops, but Cadfael gardens diligently. *"And he was indeed of a rosy russet colouring, confirmed by long years of outdoor living in both east and west ... "* (6). The expression "roses in your cheeks" compliments a person's healthful appearance. Cadfael's rosy color reinforces his role as healer and indicates his optimistic outlook.

In this tale, after losing her husband and infant within a few months, the Widow Perle sadly rents her home and land to the abbey in exchange for one white rose from her old garden. The rose must be delivered on the feast of Saint Winifred. Just before the rose rent comes due, however, the rose bush is cut down and the monk who was to deliver the rose is murdered: *"Against the north wall, the white rose-bush sagged sideways, its thorny arms dragged from the stone, its thickened bole hacked in a long, downward gash that split away a third of its weight and growth dangling into the grass"* (52). Cadfael weeds out the complications of family lineage to solve a thorny mystery that ends happily with a marriage.

Everywhere I look this summer, I see roses blooming in home gardens, at malls, in cemeteries, near churches, in industrial parks, and botanical gardens. I hear roses in songs as well: "Ramblin' Rose," "Red Roses for a Blue Lady," and "Desert Rose" float through restaurants and elevators. Roses play supporting roles in many stories and songs – too many to name here:. "Alice in Wonderland," "Beauty and the Beast," "My Love is Like a Red, Red Rose." You get the idea.

Roses, for me, are associated with St. Theresa, the Little Flower. My first grade teacher Sister Joan Kevin told us about St. Theresa (1873-1897) and her affinity for roses: "Just pray to her and she will send you roses." It was probably metaphorical for grace but I took her quite literally. I prayed and prayed for roses, then forgot all about it. My mother grew hollyhocks and violets but no roses. I wanted any color roses, but envisioned yellow roses as the grandest roses of all. Maybe it was because my father was always whistling "The Yellow Rose of Texas." A few years later we moved across town to a bigger house. On the fence rambled a rose bush with enormous thorns. The yellow flowers were magnificent. St. Theresa had answered my prayer, though it took me awhile to realize that.

Recently a neighbor gave me a small yellow rose plant. I planted it in the garden, knowing that there's not really enough sun, but hoping that there is.

Bibliography

Cunningham, Scott. *Cunningham's Encyclopedia of Magical Herbs.* St. Paul, Minnesota: Llewellyn Publishing, 1994.

De Bray, Lys. *Fantastic Garlands: An Anthology of Flowers and Plants from Shakespeare.* New York, New York: Sterling Publishing Co, 1982.

De La Tour, Shatoiya. *Earth Mother Herbal: Remedies, Recipes, Lotions, and Potions from Mother Nature's Healing Plants.* Gloucester, Massachusetts: Fair Winds Press, 2002.

DeLuca, Diana. *Botanica Erotica: Arousing Body, Mind, and Spirit.* Rochester, Vermont: Healing Arts Press, 1998.

Erlanger, Steven. "Norway Extremist Denies Guilt and Suggests He Was Not Acting Alone." *New York Times:* July 26, 2011. A1, A8.

Gordon, Jean. *The Pageant of the Rose.* Cornwall, New York: Studio Publishing, 1953.

"Jin Ying Zi." *Herbal Pearls: Traditional Chinese Folk Wisdom.* Eds. Steven Foster and Yue Chong-xi. Eureka Springs, Arkansas: Boian Books, 2008. 53-4.

Hawthorne, Nathaniel. *The Scarlet Letter.* 1850. *A Longman Annotated Edition for Developing Readers.* Ed. Gert Coleman. New York: Pearson Longman, 2008.

Lust, John. *The Herb Book.* Bantam: New York, 1974.

Perrault, Charles. "Toads and Diamonds." *The Blue Fairy Book.* Ed. Andrew Lang. Dover: New York, 1965. 274-7.

Peters, Ellis. *The Rose Rent.* New York: Mysterious Press, 1986.

Powell, Jason. "Tough Old Garden Roses" Lecture at *International Herb Association Conference,* July 16, 2011.

Reppert, Bertha. *A Taste of Herbs: History, Early Gardening, and Old Recipes.* Harrisburg, Pennsylvania: Stackpole Books, 1976.

Scott, Timothy. *Invasive Plant Medicine: The Ecological Benefits and Healing Abilities of Invasives.* Rochester, Vermont: Healing Arts Press, 2010.

Simmons, Adelma Grenier. *Saints in My Garden.* Caprilands, Connecticut. No date.

Gert Coleman luxuriating in the aroma of *Rosa.*

Gert Coleman asserts: *I love herbs, grow herbs, eat herbs, use them in crafts and read avidly about them. I read herbal mysteries, too. I give workshops and lectures on herbs and nature writing, and have 100 acres in upstate New York where my husband Peter and I are fixing up another old house and planting at-risk native plants and plenty of herbs. Associate Professor of English at Middlesex County College in Edison, New Jersey for 23 years, I live across the bay in Staten Island where I frequently walk the beach with my dog Thorne and, as a member of the S. I. Herb Society, help maintain the Colonial Herb Garden at Conference House Park.*

A lavender rose symbolizes pure love.

Rose Symbolizes Beauty

Kathleen Gips

This chapter is excerpted from: Flora's Dictionary, The Victorian Language of Herbs and Flowers by Kathleen Gips, TM Publications, 1990.

WHO, THAT HAS ever been endowed with the power of song, has not sung of the Rose? Poets have not been able to exaggerate her beauty, nor to sing her praises to perfection. They have spoken of her, and with justice, as the daughter of the sky, the ornament of the earth, and the glory of Spring; but what words have ever expressed the charms of this lovely flower, her exquisite beauty, her matchless grace? When she spreads open her petals, the eye follows her harmonious outlines with delight. But how can we describe the rounded sections which form her entirety, the lovely tints so delicately laid upon her, the sweet perfume which she sends forth? Behold her, in the Spring, raising herself softly amid her elegant foliage, surrounded by her many buds; one might say that the Queen of flowers sports with the air which plays around her, that she adorns herself with diamond-like drops of dew which bathe her, that she smiles at the sun's rays which persuade her to display her charms. Nature seems to have exhausted her resources, in order to lavish upon her to excess, freshness, beauty of form, perfume, splendour, and loveliness. The Rose decorates the whole earth; she is one of the most common flowers.

On the day that the beauty of the Rose is perfected, it begins to fade; but each succeeding Spring restores her to us fresh and new. Poets have sung of her charms in vain; they have not made her praises grow old or become wearisome; and her name of itself keeps their productions fresh and attractive. The emblem of every age; the interpreter of all our sentiments; the Rose is mixed up with our festivals, with our joys and our sorrows. Innocent mirth crowns herself with Roses; simple modesty borrows her blushing tints; and we bestow a wreath of Roses as the reward of virtue. The Rose is the image of youth, innocence, and harmless pleasure. She belongs to Venus, and even is the rival of her beauty; the Rose possesses, like her, charms more lovely than beauty. (1869)

Rose: love; genteel; pretty

Rose Meanings by Color

ROSE MEANINGS CAN be translated by color as well as by historic rose type. The author has updated rose meanings using antiquarian sources relating flowers and colors.

Coral: glory; "I admire your accomplishment"

Lavender: pure love; "My love is genuine"

Pink: grace; "You are gentle, graceful, lovely"

Red: love; desire; "I love you"

Red and white: warmth of heart; "May happiness be yours"

White: regard; "I am worthy of you"

Yellow: friendship; "I rejoice in your friendship"

> *Resplendent rose! the flower of flowers,*
> *Whose breath perfumes Olympus' bowers,*
> *Whose virgin breath of chastened dye*
> *Enchants so much our mental eye.*
>
> ---Greek poet in Tyas, 1869

Roses and Their Meanings

From *Flora's Interpreter* by Sarah Josepha Hale, 1833

Rose, Austrian, Rosa bicolor: Thou art very lovely. A genus of nearly 50 species, chiefly indigenous to Europe. A few species found in Japan and India, and nine or ten in North America.

Rose, Bridal, Rubus rosafolius: Happy love. Rose Bridal is of the genus Rubus, which includes the Bramble family. Flowers white, usually double, small and very beautiful.

Rose, Burgundy, Rosa parvifolia: Simplicity and beauty. A dwarf shrub. Leaflet fine. Flowers small.

Rose, Campion (wild, briar rose), *Agrostemna gitbago*: Love's messengers. An European genus naturalized here: found in cornfields.

Rose, Carolina, Rosa carolina: Love is dangerous. Shrubs six or seven feet high. Flowers crimson, large.

Rose, China, Rosa multiflora: Grace. Native of Japan and China. It is a shrub of luxuriant growth, flowers in clusters, said to be white in China, but here they are pink.

Rose, Chinese, Dark, Rosa semperflorens: Forsaken. Native of China, but naturalized in Europe. Leaflets of a dark shining green. Flowers solitary.

Rose, Damask, Rosa damascena: Youth, freshness. The damask or damascena rose was first brought from Asia into Greece: then it was transplanted into Italy and France. Flowers white and red.

Rose, Damask, Rosa damascena: Bashful love. Native of Syria and Damascus, though naturalized in Europe. It is deliciously sweet. Flowers a beautiful pink, verging towards a purple.

Rose, Deep-red, *Rosa rubor*: Bashful shame. This is the wild sweet rose, improved by cultivation. It is the most common species in our gardens.

Rose, Hundred-leaved, *Rosa centfolia*: Dignity of mind, pride. This magnificent rose is a native of the southern parts of Europe. The velvet rose belongs to this species. Its colors vary from crimson to pink and purple.

Rose, Moss, *Rosa muscosa*: Superior merit. Native of the south of Europe. Stem three or four feet high: flowers at the top of the branch large, very fragrant, of a bright crimson hue: flowers double.

Rosebud, Moss, *Rosa muscosa*: Confession. A rose bud just opening, according to Berkley's Utopia, is a declaration of love.

Rose, Multiflora, (bramble flowered Chinese rose): Grace.

Rose, Mundi, *Rosa versicolor*: You are merry. An American rose, being a variety of the species *lucida*. Found from New York to Carolina. Flowers elegantly striped or variegated with red and white.

Rose, Musk, *Rosa moschata*: Charming. The musk rose is exceedingly beautiful. Native of Barbary, and from its petals the essential oil is obtained, called "Otto of Roses."

Rosebud, Red, *Rosa rubrifolia*: May you ever be pure and lovely. There is no emblem more significant of youth, beauty, and innocence, than a rosebud. The rubrifolia is a native of North America.

Rose, Red-leaved, *Rosa rubrifolia*: Beauty and prosperity. Native of Switzerland and Savoy. Stem erect. The whole plant, branches, leaves, stalks and the tube of the calyx are more or less tinged with red.

Rose, Thornless, *Rosa inermis*: Ingratitude. Native of Switzerland and North America. The stem is five or six feet high, without a prickle: and Lemaistre asserts that the thorns on the other species have been produced by cultivation: hence the emblem, ingratitude. Flowers crimson.

Rose, White, Rosa alba: Sadness. The rose was sacred to Venus, and the table says, was originally white, but the goddess being wounded by a thorn, the blood "On the white rose being shed, made it forever red."

Rose, White, withered, Rosa alba: I am in despair. Native of Europe. The bush is five or six feet high. Leaves dark green. Flowers usually pure white, but sometimes tinged with a delicate blush.

Rose, Yellow, Rosa lutea: Let us forget. The yellow rose is a native of Italy. They are both single and double, and have the odor of a pineapple.

Rose, York and Lancaster, Rosa versicola: War. This species was the common dog-rose: the red adopted by the house of Lancaster, the white by that of York.

> Oh! I love the sweet blooming, the pretty moss rose,
> 'Tis the type of true pleasure, and perfected joy;
> Oh! I envy each insect that dares to repose
> 'Midst its leaves, or among its soft beauties to toy.
> I love the sweet lily, so pure and so pale,
> With a bosom as fair as the new-fallen snows;
> Her luxuriant odours she spreads through the vale,
> Yet e'en she must yield to my pretty moss rose.
> Oh! I love the gay hearts-ease, and violet blue,
> The sun-flower and blue-bell, each floret that blows,
> · The fir-tree, the pine-tree, acacia, and yew,
> Yet e'en she must yield to my pretty moss rose.
> Yes, I love my moss rose, for it ne'er had a thorn,
> 'Tis the type of life's pleasures, unmix'd with its woes;
> 'Tis more gay, and more bright, than the opening morn:
> Yes, all things must yield to my, pretty moss rose.

---Anonymous in *Flora's Lexicon*, 1839

Rose acacia: elegance

Rose, cabbage: the ambassador of love

Rose, daily: "That smile I would aspire to!"

Rose, dried: death preferable to loss of innocence

Rose, full blown: "You are beautiful"

Rose in a tuft of grass: There is everything to be gained by good company. The poet Sadi said, "One day I saw a rose-bush surrounded by a tuft of grass. What! I cried, does that vile plant dare to place itself in the company of Roses? I was about to tear the grass away, when it meekly addressed me, saying, 'Spare me! I am not the Rose, it is true; but, from my perfume, any one may know at least that I have lived with Roses.'" How anxiously should we seek the company of those whose intellectual and moral character surpasses our own, that we may drink in some of their mind's wealth and moral worth, and so far be improved by the association. (1869)

Rose leaf: "I am never importunate"

Rose, maiden's blush: "If you do love me, you will find me out"

> *I do betray myself with blushing!*
> ---Shakespeare

Rose, Moss, Rosa muscosa: Pleasure without alloy. The elegant moss rose is commonly supposed to be the offspring of the Provence rose, though some consider it to belong to the family of hundred-leaved roses. It has ever been male the emblem of perfected joy; Milton mentions it as "without thorn, the rose"; and an anonymous writer has sung of it in that character. (1839)

Rose, unique: 'Call me not beautiful"

Rose, white, withered: transient impressions

Rose, without a thorn: ingratitude

Rose, yellow: the decrease of love on better acquaintance

Rose-scented geranium: preference

Rosebud: youth; beauty; innocence; young girl

Rosebud, red: "You are young and beautiful"; "May you ever be pure and lovely"

Rosebud, white: a heart that is ignorant of love; too young to love; "The heart that knows not love"

Rose hips: the fruits of love

> Be your heart as pure,
> Your cheek as bright
> As the spring rose.

> ---Miss Loudon in Flora's Interpreter, 1833

Rose Elf

'Color Magic' is a hybrid tea rose.

Kathleen Gips has been growing, studying and writing about herbs for over twenty-five years. Her areas of herbal knowledge include aromatherapy, herbal skin care, essential oils, teas and tea service, as well as culinary, horticultural and historical uses. Her main area of research has been the tussie mussie, or herbal nosegay, and the language of herbs and flowers. She owns an extensive collection of antique posy holders and floral dictionaries that complement her research. Kathleen has had a number of articles published nationally and has been the editor of two herb publications published by The Herb Society of America. Her book, **Flora's Dictionary: The Victorian Language of Herbs and Flowers**, is now in its third printing. This work documents the use of florigraphy in the 1800s. For more info about Kathleen and her shop: <u>www.villageherbshop.com</u>

Roses—Passing through Time and Tastes

Karen O'Brien

THE ROSE, OFTEN referred to as the "Queen of Flowers," is practical, sensuous, beautiful, and revered by many. Found throughout the world, its long history of use and cultivation and its enduring nature make the rose one of the most loved of flowers.

Fossil evidence of roses dating to 32 million years ago has been uncovered in Oregon and Colorado. Petals of *Rosa ricardii* have been unearthed from Egyptian tombs, having been used in elaborate funerary bouquets from the Ptolemaic period (305 to 30 B.C.). Early Greek mythology credits the origin of the rose to the goddess of love, Aphrodite, whose birth created sea foam, which turned into white roses, signifying purity and innocence.

The survival of the rose as a plant throughout the ages was ensured by its botanic design. The five petals of simple, single roses are attractive to insects, guaranteeing pollination. The prickles, or thorns, make the foliage less likely to be decimated by browsing animals. The seedy rose hips, or fruit, are eagerly eaten by birds, and deposited far and wide through their elimination. Early man must have valued and protected the plant, as its flowers and hips and even young shoots were not only tasty, but nourishing too.

Roses are often thought of by many as a symbol of love. In the far East, the rose was considered a symbol of virtue; in Rome it symbolized festivity. Though roses were not known to be used in Egypt until later pharaonic times, the Egyptians associated the rose with silence. The custom of adorning a ceiling with roses as a reminder to never repeat anything spoken beneath (*sub rosa*) may be a usage borrowed by the Romans from the Egyptians as the Roman Empire expanded.

Roses throughout the world and through the ages have been treasured not only for their scent and flavor, but also for their medicinal and cosmetic properties. Pliny the Elder (23-79), a Roman historian and writer, wrote in his *Naturalis Historia* that charred rose petals were of great use to darken the eyebrows, and suggested that dried, powdered rose petals should be sprinkled about the body as a deodorant. Avicenna (980-1037), a Persian physician, called for rose oil in many of his healing preparations. In the Middle Ages, the apothecary rose (*R. gallica officinalis*) was extremely popular and distilled quite often. The oil was used medicinally, often to mask the unpleasant odors and tastes of the bitter types of brews and potions of the period.

The cultivation of roses, including grafting, budding and pruning, was a skill perfected by the Romans and spread across their Empire. Some early roses, such as Campanian, Milesian, Carthaginian, Paestum, Musk (*R. moschata*) and *R. gallica*, were planted and nurtured in all areas of the Roman Empire that would support their growth. The lavish use of roses for adornment, in food, and for cosmetic and medicinal use required huge amounts of flowers. It takes, for example, over 4,000 pounds of rose petals to make one pound of rose oil.

It is traditionally believed that the briar rose, (*R. canina*) was the source for the crown of thorns placed on Christ's brow at his crucifixion. It is understandable then, that in Christian flower symbolism, the rose stood for the blood of martyrs. The monk Walafrid Strabo (809-849), in his writings at the St. Gall Monastery, penned the earliest surviving record of a monastic garden. His work included the lines "roses . . . for the martyr's blood . . . His death re-dyed the roses." Many religious paintings of saints from this period depict a lily and a rose: the lily indicated purity, and the rose symbolized the blood that was shed. In Europe, a favorite medicinal potion for hemorrhaging included roses; the Doctrine of Signatures popular at the time would have concluded that something associated with or similar to blood would be good for ailments concerning blood.

The German mystic, Hildegard von Bingen (1098-1179) referred to the rose in her *Physica,* a large body of work that included healing plants.

She wrote that a rose leaf laid over an eye would draw out the "humour" and make the eye clear. Roses, she also noted, would serve to strengthen any medication to which it was added. Anthony Askham's *Herbal* (1550) provided a recipe for *Melrosette*, to be used for "*feble sycke, flumatike melancholy and colorike people.*" Boiling honey with chopped red rose petals would bring relief to those suffering, and the preparation was guaranteed to be good for five years.

The botanist John Parkinson (1567-1650) mentions roses over and over in his *Theatrum Botanicum* of 1640. A recipe for rose and cinquefoil tea appeared in the *Virginia Gazette* in 1774, claiming that it was beneficial to feverish people, good for mitigating pain and inflammation, healing wounds and recruiting strength. In *The Toilet of Flora* (1784), one is advised to bathe in a bath of vinegar of roses and borage root to remove marks on the skin, and that a preparation of red roses, sweet flag and orris root "enlivens the imagination and helps the memory."

A dichotomy of the properties of roses in ancient times is illustrated in the work of Albertus Magnus in 1502, *The Book of Secrets.* In it he speaks of the rose as capable of both inducing sterility and restoring life. This book attempted to unlock the science of magic for good and knowledge by revealing the hidden powers of herbs and other elements in nature. The fifteenth herb he listed was the rose, which needed to be combined with a mustard seed and the foot of a weasel. If this amulet were placed in a net, fish would be drawn to it. But, conversely, if the charm were placed in a tree, the tree would become barren and fruitless.

Today, roses are used in many of the same ways, following ancient traditions and methods. Rose water is used in cooking and cosmetics, rose oil can be found in perfumes, and aromatherapists use the scent of roses for emotional balance and a calming effect. We have roses in liqueurs, jams, conserves and teas. A bouquet of roses is still the flower of choice for Valentine's Day and other special occasions. In Thailand, an infusion of *Kulap Mon* (damask rose, *R. damascena*) is used as a stimulant to counter low immunity, energy and chronic fatigue. Rose hips are an excellent source of vitamin C, and wild rose hips are a good source of food for wintering animals.

The highly favored rose otto, the essential oil extracted from *Rosa damascena*, is still produced in two countries–Turkey and Bulgaria. It is interesting to note that 16th century Ottoman merchants (now known as Turkish) were responsible for bringing rose production to the Balkan country of Bulgaria. There was an area there so perfect for growing roses that Bulgaria became the leader of rose production in the world. Each year the Festival of Roses is celebrated in Kazanlik in the "Valley of Roses" during the annual harvest of roses. A Rose Queen is crowned, workers dress in traditional costume to hand pick the roses, and the sweet scent of roses perfumes the air.

The rose continues to enchant, impress and gratify. Whether you grow roses, receive them as gifts, or make or use rose products in your daily life, it is clear that roses are an important part of our world, as much if not more so than in our ancestors' lives. A scent of roses can lift your spirits, and even one rose can make one smile. Remember this quote by George William Curtis:

> *"The fragrance always stays in the hand that gives the rose."*

Bibliography

Best/Brightman, eds. *The Book of Secrets of Albertus Magnus.* New York: Oxford University Press, 1973.

Bunn, Mrs. J. Wilbur, Commission chair. *A Tryon Palace Trifle.* North Carolina: Tryon Palace Commission, 1960.

Clarkson, Rosetta E. *Green Enchantment.* New York: Macmillan Co., 1942.

_____. *Magic Gardens.* New York: Macmillan Co., 1942.

_____. *The Golden Age of Herbs and Herbalists.* New York: Dover, 1972.

de Waal, Marinus, Dr. *Medicines from the Bible.* York Beach, Maine: Samuel Wiser Inc., 1994.

Fox, Helen Morganthau. *Gardening with Herbs for Flavor and Fragrance.* New York: Dover, 1970.

Gordon, Lesley. *The Mystery and Magic of Trees and Flowers.* Exeter, England: Webb & Bower, 1985.

Hole, Christina. *The English Housewife in the Seventeenth Century.* London: Chatto & Windus, 1953.

Hozeski, Bruce W., translator. *Hildegard's Healing Plants.* Boston: Beacon Press, 2001.

Kerr, Jessica. *Shakespeare's Flowers.* New York: Thomas Y. Cromwell Co., 1969.

Manniche, Lise. *An Ancient Egyptian Herbal.* Cairo, Egypt: American University Cairo Press, 2006.

Spurling, Hilary. *Elinor Fettiplaces Receipt Book.* Harmondsworth, England: Penguin Books, 1986.

Author unknown. *The Toilet of Flora (1779),* Milford, Connecticut: Herb Lovers Book Club, 1939.

Karen O'Brien runs her herbal business "The Green Woman's Garden" in the central Massachusetts town of Mendon. She grows herbs, heirloom vegetables and ornamental flowers, runs workshops on various herbal adventures, and occasionally participates at farmers' markets and fairs. She has gardened for more than 30 years and is certified as a Master Gardener. She is the Development Chair of The Herb Society of America; currently serves as Vice Chairman of the New England Unit of H.S.A.; is Secretary of the International Herb Association; sits on the Board of the Greenleaf Garden Club of Milford; and serves as State Advocate for "Leave No Trace".

Rosa carolina, a wild woodland rose, grows in pastures or dry open woods from southern Ontario to Texas and Florida.

The Rose in Native American Cultures

Ann Sprayregen

THROUGH THE AGES, the rose has appeared in the poetry, legends, music, painting, and culinary and medical arts of the Middle East, Asia and parts of Africa. However, there is a richness of information and knowledge here in our own backyard—in the experiences, stories, practices, and art of Native Americans. This knowledge is embedded in the long oral traditions and practices of these many and varied people, causing it to be difficult to obtain. That which was known has often been kept secret, guarded and protected from misuse, exploitation, or attempts at the assimilation of Native American children into English-speaking Christian society.

There is a vast field of information and there is much for us to learn. Most important is the awakening that can come from some understanding and appreciation of the complex Native American view of the world: *All living things of this physical world possess a spirit, and the physical world and the spiritual world are inextricably interwoven.* Such a world view affects every aspect of life, including language and choice of names, as well as guides a relationship to all living things.

The preponderance of the information herein, and indeed the outline and much of the language is indebted to the carefully thought-through and knowledgeable contribution of Michael Wassegijig Price (Wikwemoikong First Nations).

Naming the Rose

WHAT IS THE Native American name for the rose? This is a simple question for those of us from a Western tradition. However, to native people, the question is more complex. It is necessary first of all to understand that the indigenous way of knowing plants differs from the scientific Linnaeus method of categorization. Local environment, other plants and animals, cultural traditions and history all enter into the naming and enable people to grasp the full significance of a name that has been given to a plant. An example is the phrase "Kishipi iminaki," meaning "to itch like hemorrhoids". This is the name the Mesawakiin of Central Iowa give to the wild rose, and refers to the bowel irritation caused by ingesting the microscopic hairs found within the rose hip fruit. The Anishinaabe word "Bizhikiwiginiig" for wild rose incorporates the smaller words meaning "buffalo" and "rose flowers". Translated as Buffalo Roses, it evokes the sight, smell, sound of the great buffalo herds plowing up the plains for the plains grasses and grazing on the various parts of the rose in their season.

Tobasonakwut Kinew, a highly respected Anishinaabe Elder, says, "The sacred knowledge of the natural world is inherent in the language." There is therefore a relationship that exists between the rose and its environment, use, etc., that dictates what it is to be called. Each name then evokes a complexity of memories, thoughts and feelings.

The Rose in Tribal Floral Design

THE ROSE IS often found among the intricate floral patterns created from dyed porcupine quills, bone beads and colorful cordage which native people used to decorate clothing. Among the most popular designs for Ojibwa beadwork are wild roses and rosebuds. Elders explain that originally the floral designs represented medicine plants. Wearing the design of a particular medicinal plant could bring power and good medicine to that individual. The rose design is often seen at Anishinaabe gatherings today.

The Rose as Medicine and Food

TRIBES ACROSS THE country have used every part of the wild rose as medicine—roots, leaves, flowers, hips and buds. Healers from the Ojibwe, Cree and Iroquois created an eye wash from the petals, stem and root bark of wild rose to relieve eye irritation and pain from snow blindness and the winter cold. Many tribes used wild rose in the treatment of open or bleeding flesh wounds. The Ojibwe created a decoction of pulverized wild rose roots to prevent bleeding by applying it directly to the wound. The Crow of central Montana created a vapor using crushed roots in boiling water to treat nosebleeds. They also used the same remedy to make a compress to reduce the swelling of skin wounds. Tawnees harvested the large hypertrophied outgrowths on the rose stem (galls), charred them in a fire and applied them, brushed into a poultice directly to the wound. People of the First Nations in British Columbia treated athlete's foot by placing rose leaves in their moccasins. Cherokee healers made a medicine bath of wild rose roots to treat babies and children with worms.

These are only a few of the myriad of treatments and cures, honed by observation and practice by the many Native American tribes over the centuries.

Every part of the wild rose plant has been used as a food source, too, by native peoples. Rose hips were considered famine food because they could be found above the snow during winter months. Leaves and flower petals were eaten raw, while roots, stems and leaves were used in making teas. Native Americans learned about the food value of various plants from animals.

An Anishinaabe legend relates the tale of a group of young warriors who came across Makwa—Black Bear— walking through the forest. The eldest of the warriors decided to kill Makwa and bring him back for a feast. In doing so, they would be renowned for their bravery and revered as great hunters. As they crept through the forest, the eldest noticed that the bear seemed to be looking for something. Makwa pulled over long, slender thorny bushes and began eating the red fruit fixed atop. They watched patiently for a good shot as Makwa gorged on these berries. Next Makwa proceeded toward the lake.

Fearing that he would get away, they began to affix their arrows onto the bear; but then they noticed him pulling up tall water grass and eating the white fleshy bulbs beneath the surface of the water. After he had gotten his fill, Makwa walked off into the forest. The young warriors quickly ran over to the bushes and ate both the red berries and the whitish bulbs. They ran back to the village and told the elders what they had witnessed. From that moment on, Makwa, the bear, was no longer regarded as a food source but as the teacher of herbs and medicines. Medicine men and women of the Anishinaabe people revere the black bear for its knowledge and wisdom, which is considered sacred.

Because of the rose's fragrance and the tastiness of its green stems, other legends have explained the necessity of providing the rose with thorns to ensure its survival.

A Salteaux story tells how Nanaboozhoo, the trickster god of the woodlands people, was angered that the rabbit and other animals had nearly decimated the wild roses around his garden. In response to the pleas of the few remaining rose bushes, he gave them a lot of small thorn-like prickles to cover their branches and stems close up to the flower.

The Rose and Native American Spirituality

RECOGNIZING THAT ALL things possess a spirit, Native Americans developed ways to communicate with the spiritual world that surrounded them. Throughout centuries of interacting with the environment, they have practiced these customs and ceremonies in daily life, the meaning and purpose of which have never been shared with Western society. They have passed on these traditions to the next generations in their stories. Herbal knowledge, ceremonies, and cultural practices relate directly to the ancestral eco-region of a particular tribe, so the spiritual landscape would be as diverse as the landscapes they inhabit. Gradually, over the years, some of the legends and practices have come into more general knowledge.

Some tribal people believe that the wild rose has a unique spirit that is deserving of respect and recognition.

A Lakota legend tells of a time when the world was young and the people had not arrived, when no flowers bloomed on the prairie. Only the grasses and dull, greenish-gray shrubs grew there. Earth felt very sad because her robes lacked brightness and beauty. "I have many beautiful flowers in my heart, I wish they were on my robe. Blue flowers like the clear sky in fair weather... brilliant yellow ones like the dawn of a spring day..." A sweet little pink flower heard Earth's sadness and said, "Do not be sad Mother Earth, I will go upon your robe and beautify it." So the little pink flower came up from the heart of Mother Earth to beautify the prairies.

But when the Wind Demon saw her, he growled, "I will not have that pretty flower on my playground." He rushed at her, shouting and roaring, and blew out her life. One after another, other flowers tried to adorn the Earth with their delicate blooms. They, too, were destroyed by the Wind, their spirits also returning to the heart of Mother Earth. At last the Prairie Rose offered to go. "Yes, sweet child," said Mother Earth, "I will let you go. You are very lovely and your breath so fragrant that surely the Wind Demon will be charmed by you. Surely he will let you stay on the prairie." So Prairie Rose made the long journey up out of the dark ground and came out on the drab prairie.

When Wind Demon saw her, he rushed at her shouting, "I will not have that pretty flower on my playground. I will blow out her life." and he rushed on, roaring and drawing his breath in strong gusts. As he came closer, he caught the fragrance of Prairie Rose. "Oh... how sweet," he said to himself. "I do not have it my heart to blow out the life of such a beautiful maiden with so sweet a breath. She must stay here with me. I must make my voice gentle and I must sing sweet songs. I must not frighten her away with my awful noise."

So Wind Demon changed. He became quiet and sent breezes over the prairie grasses. He whispered and hummed little songs of gladness. He was no longer a demon. The other flowers came up from the heart of Mother Earth through the dark ground. They made her robe, the prairie, bright and joyous. Even Wind came to love the blossoms among the grasses. And so the robe of Mother Earth became beautiful because of the sweetness and courage of the Prairie Rose.

Native Americans have persevered in the harshest of environments, adapted to rapidly changing surroundings, survived adverse conditions, and yet have maintained their beauty and essence. The relatively modern legend of the Cherokee Rose (nu na hi du na tio hi lou i) well-illustrates this, as told by "Aunt Mary":

More than 100 years ago, the Cherokee people were driven from their home when the white men discovered gold in the mountains of North Carolina and Georgia. Their journey to distant lands is remembered as The Trail of Tears. It was early summer and very hot, and most of the time the people had to walk. Tempers were short and many times the soldiers were more like animal drivers than guides for the people. The men were so frustrated with the treatment of their women and children, and the soldiers were so harsh and frustrated that bad things often happened. Men were killed and many people died of much hardship. Women wept for the loss of their homes and their dignity.

The old men knew they must do something to help the women not lose their strength in weeping. They would have to be very strong in order to help the children survive. So one night after they had made camp, they called up to the Great One in Galounati (heaven) to help the people in their trouble. They told him that the people were suffering and feared that the little ones would not survive to rebuild the Cherokee Nation.

The Great One said, "Yes, I have seen the sorrows of the women and I can help them to keep their strength to help the children. Tell the women in the morning to look back where their tears have fallen to the ground. I will cause to grow quickly a plant. They will see a little green plant at first with a stem growing up. It will grow up and up and fall back down to touch the ground where another stem will begin to grow. I'll make the plant grow so fast at first that by afternoon they'll see a white rose, a beautiful blossom with five petals. In the center I will put a pile of gold to remind them of the gold which the white man wanted when his greed drove the Cherokee from their ancestral home."

The Great One said that the green leaves will have seven leaflets, one for each of the seven clans of the Cherokee. The plant will begin to spread all over, a very strong plant, a plant which will grow in large, strong clumps and it will take back some of the land they had lost. It will have stickers on every stem to protect it from anything that tries to move it away.

The next morning, the old men told the women to look back for the sign from the Great One. The women saw the plant beginning as a tiny shoot and grow-

ing up and up until it spread out over the land. They watched as a blossom formed, so beautiful they forgot to weep, and they felt beautiful and strong. By the afternoon they saw many white blossoms as far as they could see. The women began to think about the strength given them to bring up their children as the new Cherokee Nation. They knew the plant marked the path of the brutal Trail of Tears. The Cherokee women saw that the Cherokee Rose was strong enough to take back much of the land of their people.

This small, thorny flowering bush often inspired healers to cure the ill, quelled hunger during times of struggle, created humorous stories and fables that would live for generations, nourished the body and lifted the spirits of the oppressed. The rose's place in the traditions and customs of Native Americans is undeniably entrenched and intertwined with the spiritual nature of its people.

Sources

Michael Wassegijig Price (Wikwemoikong First Nations): 'Wild Roses and Native Americans', the first article in *Rose Lore, Essays in Cultural History and Semiotics*, edited by Frankie Hutton., 2008 In his bibliography, Dr. Price lists all the sources from which he has drawn information for his article.

"Aunt Mary": *Aunt Mary, Tell Me A Story*. A Collection of Cherokee Legends and Tales as Told by Mary U. Chiltosky

Ann Sprayregen was Associate Professor at NYC College of Technology (CUNY). She retired from there, where she worked with the College Discovery and SEEK Programs. Her longtime interest in herbs and health foods first lead her introduce the SHARE Food Program into the college community, and then, together the parents and staff of the defunded daycare center, sell herbs and health foods to the captive audience—a great learning experience for all.

'Dr. W. van Fleet' is a rose prized for its fragrance.

Favorites

Rosa 'Betty Prior' is Jane Taylor's favorite for its continuous blooms.

A Collection of Favorite Roses

Susan Belsinger

I queried the members of the IHA and other herbal/gardening colleagues to send me their favorite roses and tell me why they are their favorites in a few sentences and up to a paragraph. Some were succinct and others revealed a passion for roses; not just one. Here are the responses that I received.

Rosa '**Betty Prior**' is a single floribunda, introduced in 1935. It blooms continuously from June to frost and is hardy to Zone 4. It is lovely in cottage gardens, has three-season interest and is fragrant. Height is 2-to 5-feet and up to 5-feet wide. The single blooms are carmine pink.

---Jane L. Taylor

Sentimentally, I have a '**Cherokee**' rose that has been in my family for unknown years. It is thought a clipping was brought on the Trail of Tears by a family member or a clipping from one that had been. The small blossom is heavy with a wonderful fragrant perfume.

The **Knock Out**® rose has become my favorite due to its hardiness and constant blooms throughout our hot and often dry summers. Even the Japanese beetles cannot destroy them.

---Kay Whitlock

I love the '**Double Delight**' rose best for a lot of reasons; I was selling bare-root roses bushes while working at my family's nursery the year it was introduced in 1977 (also happens to be the year I graduated from high school) and I am unabashedly sentimental. (Another rose I favor happens to be '**Scentimental**' for almost all the same reasons as '**Double Delight**.') '**Double Delight**' was given the All-American Rose selection award that year.

I read that it was inducted into the World Rose Hall of Fame in 1985 which squares with my memory because I was still selling roses at my cousin's nursery then, as well as later when the patent on the rose expired in 1997. Once a patent expires anyone can sell the rose without paying royalties to the hybridizer and/or patent holder and this was a big deal in the industry with regards to '**Double Delight**' since it was and still is, an all-time, best-selling rose. It is a cross between two other favorite roses of mine, '**Garden Party**' and '**Granada**' and, not only does it boast gorgeous dual colors, it also has a sublime, quintessential rose fragrance. What's not to like?

---Karen England

Rosa 'Heritage' is Holly Shimizu's choice for herbal use.

For herbal use my favorite rose is **Rosa 'Heritage'** because it is long blooming, fragrant, and has many pink petals. Of equal importance, it does not need any spraying so the petals can be used safely for food, flavor, and fragrance.

As a garden plant my favorite rose is **Rosa 'Madame Pavie'** because she is small (about 3 feet), has beautiful form, stunning buds that are pale pink, and petals that turn to white as the flowers open. Her perfume is divine.

---Holly Shimizu

My favorite is **'Mme. Hardy'** with her wonderful damask rose fragrance, brilliant flowers, and envious green eye.

---Art Tucker

Polyantha rose, *Rosa* 'Marie Pavie', has a divine perfume.

Rosa rugosa gets two votes for favorite rose.

Rosa 'Tuscany' is an extremely hardy old rose.

Rosa rugosa is my favorite rose, hands down. For the simplicity of its bloom, its color and its fragrance, and for the handsome bright green, deeply-veined foliage, it is an all-around beautiful specimen. Its aromatic bright, dark-pink petals are superior in the kitchen and *boudoir*, having a strong, yet not overpowering, long-lasting, deep rose perfume and taste. The hips are quite large and showy and I use them both for culinary and medicinal preparations. The **Apothecary rose** (*R. gallica*) is a close runner up—for appearance, fragrance and use.

---*Susan Belsinger*

Also known as Japanese Wild Rose, **Rosa rugosa** is my choice for favorite rose. This is the most trouble-free, vigorous, historic rose I've grown. My friend, Ruth Smith, gave me a start and I've used its fragrant, colorful petals to make rose waters, syrups, (dried) in ice cubes, Elizabethan body and glove powders, potpourris, as well as in the bottom of cup and cake-baked batters.

---*Pat Kenny*

'Tuscany' is my favorite rose because everybody has it and nobody planted it. I've heard numerous people say, "I have two different color flowers on the same rose bush"—just before they lose the rose that they originally bought. Tuscany is one of the oldest Gallica roses and is extremely hardy, thus it has been used for grafting for years. It generally outlasts the graft and reverts back to red or dark red blooms, which are quite pretty and smell good too.

---*Deborah Hall*

I am taking the liberty here, to speak of one of Adelma Simmons' favorite roses—because it made such an impression upon me. On my first visit to Capriland's Herb Farm in the late 70s, I happened to go there on the day of the summer solstice, not realizing there was a Midsummer celebration afoot. Well of course the farmhouse was decorated—filled with every variety of herbs, flowers and roses—and everyone got to wear a crown of herbs made from the symbolic mugwort and vervain entwined. Since roses were abundantly in bloom, Adelma had made a crown of **'Dr. W. van Fleet'** roses, which she wore upon her head. As we drank our titillating punch, Adelma waxed poetic about the beauty and fragrance of the '**Dr. W. van Fleet**' rose and took the breathtaking crown from her head to pass around for us all to admire and inhale the perfume.

I don't recall how or why—perhaps it was the light pink shirt that I had worn which matched the rose—however, I got to wear the crown of palest pink, full-blown flowzy roses and it made me practically loopy with the fragrance (could have had something to do with her punchbowl ingredients). I will never see or smell this rose without bringing that magical day and one of our great herbal mentors to mind.

---Susan Belsinger remembering Adelma Grenier Simmons

'Dr. W. van Fleet' was a favorite rose of Adelma Grenier Simmons.

My Mother's Roses

Lucia Ferrara Bettler

I STARTED GARDENING as a young bride in the '70s. My gardens have always been a solace and a comfort, a place to dig and sweat, and kneel on the damp earth and work out life's frustrations. My journey to gardening began years before in my mother's garden, or "yard" as she called it.

Mama had many flower beds, always blooming with something luscious, always brimming with floral riches. There were crimson Miranda roses, apricot tea roses, flowering plum and kumquat trees, Easter lilies, Louisiana iris, lycoris and tiny fragrant carnations whose clove-like scent I will never forget. There was mint for her tea and basil and oregano for her spaghetti sauce.

We would tour her gardens as if they were the Garden of Versailles, instead of an Italian immigrant's earthly treasure. Her plump tomatoes and eggplant were right next to the roses, and fennel sprang up around all of them. She always had basil seeds coming up in an old olive oil can, and coffee cans full of rose cuttings or velvety red coxcomb. Her yard was my haven and retreat, and the first sacred place I knew.

Her parents, Maria and Guiseppe Loverde, were from Sicily, and as farmers, were people of the soil and the earth. She learned how to grow just about anything from them when they lived in Dickenson, Texas before 1916. Later they all moved to Houston, where every one of my aunts and uncles had backyard gardens... filled with vegetables and flowers.

When I see roses, I always think of my mother, Santina, or "Tena" as she was called. They were her favorite flower. She always made bouquets to bring into the house. She would dry gallons of rose petals for me in her dining room, so I could make my Earth Rose Potpourri. The last fifteen years of her life she wore a Tea Rose fragrance, and it matched the rosy bloom in her cheek that was there well into her later years. Her room was decorated with a small, rose-patterned throw and we always gave her china and stationery decorated with them.

Her most favorite rose was a small "sweetheart" rose that started out a peachy-apricot color and fully bloomed into a paler pink. When she dried them, they turned almost burgundy and had the most fragrant scent! We never knew the real name, until I was speaking at the Antique Rose Emporium in Brenham years later. While looking at all the roses, I saw it! "There's Mama's rose !" I exclaimed to Henry Flowers.

I learned it was the Perle d' Or rose, a China hybrid from 1884 France. It was like peaches and cream and always brought us such delight, sometimes as many as 30 blossoms covering its lush green bush. It was her favorite and now it is mine. This rose is a vision, in a tiny pitcher or vase, mixed with some shiny green rosemary. Now I have three of the bushes, blooming near my kitchen door, and when they bloom, I feel my mother's arms wrapped around me.

Lucia Ferrara Bettler has been passionate about herbs and gardening for over 25 years. A native Houstonian and a former English teacher, she is the owner of Lucia's Garden, a well known Houston gift/herbal shop and learning center that strives to nourish the body as well as the spirit. Her knowledge of herbs, her love for travel, and extensive mythological and folkloric research adds a rich dimension to Lucia's teaching. Her business blossomed from her connection to the earth, first through her interest in potpourri and then through her study and use of culinary and medicinal herbs. She is a member of the Herb Society of America and is a past president of the International Herb Association. www.luciasgarden.com

My Favourite Rose

Pat Crocker

At FIRST BLUSH, one might describe my favorite rose as 'butter yellow' or 'whipped lemon mousse' or even as being 'a frothy apricot and lemon confection'. That's because my favorite rose is 'Julia Child' and because it was named in honor of one of America's most beloved foodies, I couldn't help but think of food–ingredients, beverages and desserts–when I discovered it at Bellingrath Gardens in Alabama.

Bending my nose to the full and fluted, English-style rose I was immediately transported not only to the kitchen, but also to the old-fashioned candy store where at one time hundreds of licorice candies were on display. And while the sweetly anise scent was the first to reach my aroma receptors, after that a lightly spiced overtone registered and to my delight, I was alongside Julia herself as she beat anise into *Pain D'Epices* (Spice Cake, page 481) from Volume II of her now famous cookbook, *Mastering the Art of French Cooking*.

The 'Julia Child' rose is a floribunda rose and an All-America Rose Selection for 2006. According to The AARS official Web site http://www.rose.org/2006-winner-julia-child/, "This rose has a rounded habit and excellent disease resistance … (and) … a butter-gold color that's perfectly suited to any landscape."

The bonus for me is that I can grow it here in Canada because it is hardy to Zone 4 with winter protection! Isn't it just like Julia to personally select a rose with international appeal?

Read *Pat Crocker*'s bio on page 36.

Pat Crocker's favorite rose 'Julia Child' looks good enough to eat!

A Visit to a Shady Lady

Terry Hollembaek

As you leave the OK Corral and saunter back towards the center of Tombstone, Arizona, you will not pass many side streets; the town just isn't that big. Down one of those short little streets you will find the Shady Lady. The time I visited her, there was a desert-browned ancient lady in bonnet and gingham blue dress collecting a dollar from each caller. I've heard the visitation fee has gone up quite a bit since then, but, trust me, the Shady Lady is worth whatever you're asked to dig out of your saddle bag. I'm only sorry that I was never able to visit her when she puts on her finery once a year in April. She is said to be even more gorgeous then and her perfume intoxicating. I'm sure that's true.

The Shady Lady is a rose. To be precise, she is a white 'Lady Banks' Rose (*Rosa banksiae*). They call her Shady Lady because she nearly covers an entire Spanish-style enclosed courtyard. She was brought to the wilds of the Wild West as a gift to a homesick Scottish bride.

She arrived in the Arizona desert in 1885 where the bride and her good friend planted and cared for her. She has prospered! The trellis work is about 8-feet high and the courtyard is much more comfortable for the shade she provides. The truly impressive, jaw-droppingly-so, feature is the trunk where she erupts from the hard-packed sandy earth. My memory is pretty good although I may be prone to exaggeration. I recollect a grape-like twisted trunk the size of a horse's neck. I could only stare, and stare and stare. The Shady Lady is one very impressive rose.

I tell anyone who mentions going to Arizona, especially herbies, "rose-philes", master gardeners and such to make a visit to the Tombstone Rose if they're even close. One friend sent me a post card with a photo of the rose when she visited and only wrote "Holy Shit!" for the message. Another friend I'd sent that way, who works with roses all summer, called me while standing beneath her and said the same thing only he said it over and over.

I could miss Boot Hill, the touristy gee-gaws, the OK Corral and the rest of Tombstone but if I even get close I'm going to visit Lady Banks, the Tombstone Rose.

Reference

www.tombstonetimes.com/stories/rose.html

Jerry Hollembaek Alaskan farm kid. Freshman teacher illuminated the world. Completed high school in the Marine Corps. Vietnam. Eclectic college career. Varied work life, Major Plant Freak. Love self learning. Love Nancy. Love music. Love life. Love History. Love Kids. Love Herbs in my life. Love writing. Love poetry. Love dressing in Historic costumes and talking to people. Built own home. Feel very, very rich. Am growing (+or-) 200 varieties of herbs. Don't own a lawn mower. Copious mulching makes my life easier and makes my Wisconsin gardens glow.

Jim Long's Favorite Roses

Jim Long

THESE ARE THE more fragrant roses I've found and photographed:

'**Amber Queen**' floribunda rose (All-American Rose Selection 1988)

'**Aztec Gold**' hybrid tea rose (very pleasing flavor)

'**Benjamin Britten**' shrub rose (sweetly flavorful)

'**Double Delight**' hybrid tea rose (delicious and fragrant)

'**Graham Thomas**' climber rose (produces an abundance of delicious, fragrant yellow, double roses)

'**Julio Iglesias**' floribunda rose (dainty, delicious flavor and fragrance)

'**Luscious**' hybrid tea rose (delicious; this is excellent for cakes and salads)

'**Mary Margaret McBride**' hybrid tea rose (All-American Rose Selection 1943)

'**Madame Joseph Schwartz**' shrub rose (deliciously scented)

'**Mister Lincoln**' hybrid tea rose (moderate flavor/fragrance for a red rose)

'**Peach Parfait**', Species rose (excellent in sandwiches and butters)

'**Perfume Delight**' hybrid tea rose (All-American Rose Selection 1974, this is an outstanding pink rose for eating!)

'Playboy' floribunda rose (a temptingly delicious fragrance and enchanting flavor)

'Scentimental' ever-blooming, floribunda rose (delicious in cakes and teas)

Wild beach rose, *Rosa rugosa* (these are prolific all summer, with a continuous supply of large, flavorful rose hips)

Jim Long's favorite red rose is 'Mister Lincoln'.

Jim Long has been eating flowers from his garden since early grade school. At age 13 he cajoled his fellow 4-H club members, boys and girls both, to choose "Cooking" as a club project. That year he subjected the entire club to tasting roses, sweet pea blossoms, violets and more. He's been cooking with herbs and flowers ever since. Jim is the author of over 2 dozen of his "Great Little Herb Books" and he is a frequent conference lecturer.

You will find how-to videos for cooking with herbs on his **YouTube/ longcreekherbs** *channel. His garden adventures can be found at* <u>jimlongsgarden.blogspot.com</u> *and postings about Herb of the Year™ can be followed at* <u>herboftheyear.blogspot.com</u>. *Visit his Web site* <u>www.LongCreek-Herbs.com</u> *for all of his books and products.*

Folk Roses

Tina Marie Wilcox

ROSES GROWING IN the Heritage Herb Garden at the Ozark Folk Center State Park in Mountain View, Arkansas have to be tough. We don't have enough gardeners to coddle fussbudgets that need sprays and constant deadheading, nor would we want to expend time on these activities.

The first tame rose here was planted in the Country Herb Garden, the very first garden at the park. It was a *Rosa rugosa* that produced single, fragrant, pink flowers and huge hips. Petals from that bush were collected, after the dew dried, and were placed in single layers on glass panes layered with about an inch of lard. This was a messy experiment in the making of pomade or *effleurage*. By afternoon, the lard, together with the carefully placed petals, melted off of the glass that sat in the hot Herb Cabin. So, it came to pass that the wooden floor of the cabin was infused with the scent of roses and lard for quite a spell.

The next experiment was a little more successful. An enamel canner half full of water was covered and set over a low-burning wood fire at the Soap Shed for a full day. Rose petals were left to simmer in the water until they lost their color. The petals were then filtered out of the liquid and fresh petals were added before the pot was set over the coals once again. Four batches of petals were simmered and filtered out in this way. The result was fragrant, dark brown rose water, which was frozen in canning jars so that it would not go bad. The rose water was used for herbal cosmetic programs until the freezer went out.

One day, long ago, a very old woman paid us a visit. As we stood admiring the *Rosa rugosa*, she confessed that during World War II she had hoarded meat grease instead of turning it in for the war effort. She said she spread it under her rosebushes and that they were lovely. Not knowing quite

This pass-along rose was planted by Mrs. Ida Branscum outside the Herb Cabin at the Ozark Folk Center.

what to say, I went on with life. During this auspicious rose year, I took the opportunity to research the woman's use of grease to understand why she would have done such a thing. I found a reference on the gardening site, http://www.gardenbanter.co.uk/australia/165519-thrips-torment-ing-me.html which said that thrips can be blocked from climbing on to rose canes with a band of grease and that the insects will flock to dishes of oil and drown. If anyone knows more about this practice, please get in touch through one of the Web sites listed below.

Finally, the *Rosa rugosa* died of crown gall, *Agrobacterium tumefaciens* *which grows like cancer on the canes and infects the soil.* I pruned out dis-eased canes for two or three years, but to no avail. Grease would not have helped. No roses will ever be planted in that garden again.

Old-time gardeners taught us to root rose cuttings under big glass jars. After stripping all but the uppermost leaves off of 4-to-6 inch, half-woody stems, we would stick them into moistened soil, on the north side of a building where the sun would not shine through the glass and burn the plants. When new growth was noticed, we would pot the cuttings for a little while to develop a root ball that would survive in the garden. This propagation method worked just fine as long as the cuttings did not have flowers on them.

A red-blooming rosebush with canes that grow straight up to about 5-feet tall grows at the doorway of what was once the Spinning Cabin. The spinner, Mrs. Ida Branscum brought the old rose from her family's farm. Because of these origins we call it "The Branscum Rose". The build-ing is now the Herb Cabin. The Branscum rose repeat blooms as long as it gets enough water, usually well into November.

When the Heritage Herb Garden was planted in 1985, two little 'The Fairy' rose bushes were a part of the show and they still live here. They are polyantha shrub roses, cultivars which were registered in 1932. They bear clusters of small, pink flowers that are not particularly fragrant. The plants are disease resistant and bloom almost all summer if not set back by extreme heat and drought. 'The Fairy' has bouts of powdery mildew, but the plants get over it without much human intervention except for severe pruning every couple of years. They are not sprayed with any-thing so that we can use the flowers for decorating cakes.

'The Fairy' rose

'Dr. W. van Fleet' is a raucous caning rose that we grew from a pass-a-long cutting many years ago. The canes of this hardy, disease-resistant plant shoot up easily to 15-feet in one season and will sprout roots wherever they bend down and touch the earth. Our specimen charms everyone with its pale pink, fragrant flowers every year on Mother's Day. The rest of the year the nicest thing we can say is that 'Dr. W. van Fleet' will keep marauders a safe distance from any place it is growing. However, my Aunt Janie, a retired-but-not-cured Rose Rustler from New Orleans, managed to steal a cutting or three when she came to speak at the Heritage Herb Spring Extravaganza this year. The popular and similar in appearance 'New Dawn' is a pink, repeat-blooming, climbing cane rose which sports from 'Dr. W. van Fleet'.

A large-flowered, modern climbing rose, 'Don Juan', was donated to the Heritage Herb Garden by textile artist, Glenda Hershberger in honor of Ray "Pop" Ramsey, schoolmaster. 'Don Juan' has semi-double, dark wine-red petals and a nice aroma. The plant is tough, disease resistant and everblooming. It gets greasy mop water most every night from the Skillet Restaurant.

Pop Ramsey had the reputation of being the best rose gardener in all of Stone County. He always fed his roses with diluted liquid fertilizer from a hose-end sprayer whenever he watered. Pops also said "If you want good roses you should always prune them back to 14-inches on February 14". His daughter Bette Rae Miller, and granddaughter Melody Miller, carry on his love for roses at the Ozark Folk Center to this very day.

'Dr. W. van Fleet' is a beautiful, pale pink climber.

Tina Marie Wilcox aiding and abetting rose-rustler Aunt Janie.

Tina Marie Wilcox almost qualifies as an old-timer in the Heritage Herb Garden at the Ozark Folk Center where she has labored with love and every other emotion since 1984. Find out about the plethora of educational and recreational opportunities at www.ozarkfolkcenter.com and www.tinamariewilcox.com.

Miscellany

Rosa spp. range from miniature six-inch bushes to thirty-foot climbers.

The Empress and the Rose

Terry Hollembaek

NAPOLEON BONAPARTE WAS very upset with his Josephine. She had arranged to buy the estate at Malmaison while he was off soldiering, beating up on Egypt. The chateau was old, run down, vastly over priced and, to top it off, she expected him to use 300,000 francs from his campaign against the land of the sphinx, to pay for it. The fact that she had been unfaithful while he was gone added one more straw to the camel's overloaded hump. Napoleon Bonaparte became very, very grumpy. In truth, furious might be a better description if writers of the time are to be trusted.

Then he forgave her, coughed up the cash to pay for the place, hired Charles Percier and Pierre Fontaine, the epitome of *avant garde* architects to give the place a serious, expensive and over-the-top redo and granted her an allowance of 40,000 francs a year.

Napoleon Bonaparte, the artillery-man-made-good, surely loved his Josephine! And the estate called Malmaison or "ill-fated domain"—because a residence of the upper echelon had been ransacked and leveled there by Vikings in 846—was perhaps his only lasting beneficial gift to the world. Almost 200 years after he himself had met his literal and metaphorical Waterloo, Malmaison and the work done there lives on in art, in our gardens, and in our appreciation of beauty in the world of plants.

Josephine loved roses! She collected as no rose collector had ever collected. De Pronville had said there were somewhere around 182 roses, but lovely, dark-haired Josephine quickly exceeded that number. "The beautiful Indian" Empress Josephine also gathered well known rose growers about her including the past director of the Luxembourg Gardens, one of the earliest growers to produce hybridized rose seeds, the eminent André DuPont.

And she began to collect plants, not just roses, as only an empress could. She was a one-of-each kind of collector and a specimen of each was her goal. She persuaded her little emperor to have every naval captain search captured enemy ships and confiscate (i.e. steal) all plants and seeds, especially roses. She spent a whopping 2,600 pounds in English sterling to import roses, including the 'Duchess of Portland' and a collection of China Roses from the English firm of Kennedy and Lee. This was in the middle of a war, yet the British Admiralty and the French military granted a pass of safe-conduct to Kennedy who delivered them and then worked for Josephine and planted them on her 150 acre estate. It was good to be the Empress!

No other plant collector in history had quite as much cash, power and pull. Only queens of ancient Egypt had collected plants with anything approaching the same well-heeled fanaticism and they didn't have the advantage of having a husband who would order all seagoing vessels to raid ships that were in the process of making the unknown world known; ships that were exploring and exploiting the lands and plants, the peoples of every far-off nation, culture and ecosystem. Josephine de Beauharnais gathered 260 different roses and grew as many as 200 assorted non-native plants in France for the first time. As a plant collector it was good to be the Empress!

Because of Josephine roses became the "in" thing. Not even the countess of Bougainville could keep up, but all of the upper class got into growing roses; the upper echelons of English society as well. And, remember, these English barons and lords and such are getting into this French fad in the middle of their war with the self-same-Francophiles. It was good to be upper class and rich regardless of which nation to which you claimed allegiance.

Josephine did not limit her extravagant collecting to roses and other plants. She also collected animals. If it was exotic and she could get it, she got it. Emus, ostriches, zebras, a seal, antelopes, black swans, gazelles and chamois along with an orangutan trained to wear human clothing all wandered freely about the grounds of Malmaison. But it was more than just collecting that got done at Malmaison. Research and experimentation were also on the priority list. Techniques for pruning, reducing bud count to force larger flowers, fertilization, wintering-over and grafting as well as some of the earliest methods of seed hybridization were developed or improved upon at Malmaison.

Then Josephine, wanting to make sure her incredible collection was recorded for all posterity, put one of the best plant artists of the day on her staff. Pierre-Joseph Redoute had spent some of his past at the beck and call of Queen Marie Antoinette as artist to her court so his credentials and his talent as well as his ability to survive guillotine fever were unimpeachable. His three-volume set *Les Roses* became, and still is, a rosephile-who-is-a-bibliophile's prized reference source. The illustrations such as 'Blush Noisette' are considered some of the best "plant art" ever created.

It was indeed good to be the Empress, but they are human too. Although she had the cash to try growing 300 tropical pineapples inside in cold winter France, and paying to fire a battery of 12 coal stoves to heat her greenhouses she, like all plant lovers, was human. In 1814 she died.

Her legacy, as far as roses goes, is staggering! What DuPont and others learned at Malmaison was spread across Europe and the world. People who were trained there scattered about France, even as the estate was falling into ruins, and started rose nurseries of their own. And the rose, always a popular flower to begin with, became a symbol of all things perfect and wondrous that every gardener, wealthy or poor had to have in their garden. True, today it is more often a tea rose than the damask rose which Josephine wore in her hair but the tea rose has its "roots" in the hybridizing done at Malmaison. Josephine had collected 260 different roses but in the 1850s, 6,000 varieties were reported and as early as 1815, scarcely a year after her passing, a man named Vibert helped a rose hybridizer named Descement sneak 10,000 rose seedlings into the countryside as Paris was occupied by the advancing victorious army. Every rose fancier and most brides and all florists owe her homage. The rose of Malmaison and the rose experts of Malmaison absolutely and indelibly changed the rose. They gave us the knowledge to diversify and change its very nature and appearance. And Josephine, because she was the Empress, made it more popular than it had ever been; a popularity that exists to this day.

It is said that Josephine de Beauharnais, Empress of France, ex-wife of Napoleon (the divorce left her owning Malmaison with a mere five million francs a year as a settlement) caught a "chill" that led to her death while walking in her gardens one evening. Why would a rich, rich lady with a beautiful warm mansion and a luxurious bedroom with a tent-like canopy over a soft featherbed be out wandering on a cold evening? Perhaps a rose variety she had never seen was getting ready to bloom; its swollen bud just beginning to show a color the Empress had never seen before. Perhaps DuPont was with her as they squinted in the twilight trying to discern the color, the texture, the character of a brand new variety of rose. I'd like to think so!

Bibliography

www.amycorwin.com/malmaison.htm
www.floralibrary.com/flora/centifolia/seedling
http://en.wikipedia.org/wiki/Ch%C3%A2teau_de_Malaison
http://en.wikipedia.org/wiki/Rueil-Malaison
http://www.georgianindex.net/Napoleon/Malmaison/Malmaison.html
www.napoleon.org/en/magazine/museums/files/National_Museum_
     the_Chateau.asp
www.letsgarden.info/info/botanic/french-rose-growers.html

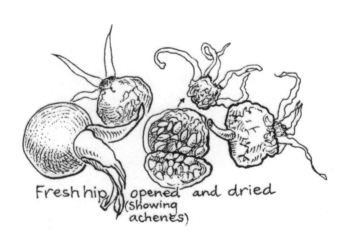

Fresh hip, opened and dried (showing achenes)

Read *Jerry Hollembaek*'s bio on page 96.

Is It A Hip, Hep, Haw, or Hypanthium?

A Review of the Literature about Rose Hips

Pat Kenny

MUCH OF WHAT we know about vitamin C-rich rose hips is common knowledge and repeated from one source to another. For this small article I prefer to refer to a few sources I know, think, or hope have been well-documented with the intention that some information may be enlightening to the reader. It is also good to know what information the general public may be accessing.

Most species roses are single-flowered, have fleshy fruit often called hips, which ripen in the late summer to autumn and are harvested after being softened by a hard frost. Nearly all references imply that it is known as a hip only when it reaches ripeness, fresh or dried. Others reveal that hip comes from the word *hypanthium* which is considered to be the concave receptacle, the floral cup just below the rose flower which develops and encloses its fruit, therefore, the fleshy tissue (2, 7). Perhaps the name changes as the botanical part matures. In our first botany class, we are often taught the flower parts attach to something called the receptacle; the receptacle bears some or all of the parts.

Most references assume that the word hip refers to the enclosure, with or without the seeds, of *Rosa canina*/Dog rose and *R. rugosa*/Rugose or Ramanas rose (13) or Tomato rose (6); some include *R. centifolia*/Cabbage rose as a major source, as well (6, 15). Hip is most commonly used, *hep* occurs enough to confuse some of us, and you may also see the term *cynarrhodion* which comes from the Greek *kyon*, dog and *rhodon*, rose (2), no matter from what species the hip comes. Although several sources I perused refer to the fruit of the rose as a haw, others say fruits of the genus

Crataegus/Hawthorn are more correctly called haws (2). The dictionaries and glossaries do not agree on hip or haw for roses. In any case, when you order hips from an herb supplier you are most likely to receive those of *R. canina*; you may be able to specify, with or without seeds.

Sepals, petals and stamens (the latter are the pollen–producing male parts) are attached to the margins of the floral cup (2, 4). After the flower is pollinated, it normally has to be fertilized before it will produce fruits and seeds. When pollen grains land on the top of the stigmas (female parts) of the same species, they germinate to produce pollen tubes which grow through the stigmas down the styles to fertilize the ovules. The ovules mature to form bony-hard achenes or, as the Brits say, *pips*, technically the aggregates of fruits or seeds inside the rose hip (5, 4). Maybe that's why I've seen rose hips called *false fruits* or *Rosae pseudofructus*. Without the stony *true fruits*, the achenes, they are considering the fleshy *hypanthia*, rose hips, as the false fruits (3).

Trichomes are the fine bristles surrounding the achenes and are best separated out with the achenes if the hips are to be processed to a more liquid state (3). Sepals are the protective green cover over an unopened rosebud; they fold back when petals are ready to unfurl (2, 4). Rose prickles, (not thorns) are woody epidermal outgrowths occurring randomly in the internodes of the stem, leaves and fruit of some species; some are curved downward and are thought to serve as a deterrent to climbing pests. Botanically, thorns are pointed reduced branches involving more layers than the epidermis (5). Stipules are outgrowths from the base of a leaf petiole and sometimes also act as a protective device.

Many rose species have hips that are edible, have a cranberry or tomato-like taste (7, 12) and are nutritious, as long as they have not been sprayed or been given a systemic chemical treatment to resist fungal or insect damage. Keep chilled after picking to inhibit formation of vitamin-destroying enzymes; process as soon as possible (1, 7).

Of the 37 roses listed as edible in *Cornucopia II*, 21 include the use of the vitamin C-rich rose hips (6).

How Rose Hips are Prepared and Used

- In China, unripe hips are peeled and cooked before eating (6).
- When ripe, eaten raw in salads, sandwich fillings, puddings and other desserts.
- Made into purees, sauces, and syrups; used in or on dairy products and baked goods.
- Stewed in a non-reactive pot (no copper or aluminum) and preserved into jams, jams with cream cheese for tea cakes (13), jellies, marmalades, and are candied.
- Dried and used in soups, in teas, herbal preparations, and added to beverages.
- Processed into wines, vinegars and sweetmeats (1, 6).
- Dried and ground to a powder for waffles and pancakes.
- The hard, bitter seeds (rich in vitamin E) can be ground and boiled in a small amount of water; the strained liquid can be added to recipes using rose hips (7).
- As a food supplement for humans, chinchillas, guinea pigs and horses; the latter receives one tablespoon per day in food for a healthier coat and stronger hooves (14).

Note: Vitamin workers have reported asthma-like symptoms from inhaling powdered rose hips (13).

Rose Hips and Vitamin C

IT IS NOT easy to hear the words *rose hips* without thinking vitamin C (ascorbic acid). During World War II, submarines were intercepting ships that were bringing in citrus, so newspaper campaigns suggested the public collect and use rose hips in their food. Peter Gail tells that his source says the Ministry of Health organized County Herb Committees into volunteers who picked tons of hips which were converted to syrup, sent to servicemen and given to children to ward off scurvy. One would think the amount of vitamin C in a hip would vary according to species, climate and cultivation. Indeed Gail admits that saying British food scientists found that hips from north of Scotland had 10 times more vitamin C than those from the south of England; and they realized that the hips needed to be processed quickly to preserve the vitamin C (7).

Tucker & DeBaggio tell us that under ideal cultural conditions rose hips may have 0.5% vitamin C (13). Many references differ saying rose hips are high in vitamin C or that they are relatively low; although, in tea, rose hip C is said to be more easily absorbable by the human body (12). A couple of sources seem to be refreshingly honest as to whether the amounts in rose hips and oranges are equivalent—how many hips = how many oranges? Hard to say.

Stein lists what are thought to be the usual chemical contents of a hip, for instance: vitamins C, E, K, beta-carotene, pectin and bioflavonoid (see Leung & Foster for more details (8)); 3-ounces of dried rose hips contain 1,700 mg. vitamin C (easily taken in 1 to 2 tablets from a health food store), actually a higher amount of vitamin C than citrus juice…often included in vitamin C formulas…used as herbal aspirin…for many of the same things (12). Large doses of vitamin C (more than 2,000 mg daily) can cause diarrhea (9).

How Rose Hips are Used Medicinally

- Anti-inflammatory, anti-oxidant, astringent, diuretic (12).
- Said to be effective for osteoarthritis as an inflammatory and pain reliever (3, 12, 14).
- Reduces joint stiffness and promotes flexibility, especially for hips and knees.
- Tones the vascular system, reduces cholesterol and blood pressure, may help prevent heart disease.
- Diuretic, relieves water retention, flushes kidneys, helps prevent cystitis and urinary tract infection symptoms, dissolves urinary gravel and kidney stones.
- Aids digestion, reduces hunger cravings for weight loss, eases constipation, diarrhea and dysentery.

- Balances intestinal flora, balances the acid-alkaline state of the body.
- Clears bronchial passages of congestion and mucus, used for colds, flu, sore throat and allergies.
- Cools body to reduce fever, helps prevent infections, boosts the immune system and thymus function.
- Protects from cancer, protects from environmental pollutants, blood cleanser.
- Aqueous and ethanol extracts of dried ramanas, *R. rugosa* flowers (presumably attached to hips) have been shown to have HIV-1 reverse transcriptive inhibitory activity (13).
- Used for headaches, dizziness, nervous tension, mastitis, uterine cramps, reduces menstrual flow and vaginal discharge; calms the fetus in the womb.
- Used in skin preparations and cosmetics to stimulate collagen growth, speeds wound and bruise healing and soothes skin irritations, rashes, burns, eczema and aging skin (12).
- Organic, cold-pressed and unrefined rose hip seed oil (from ripe hips of *R. rubiginosa*) used as body care oil is ideal for weathered skin, scars, wrinkles; keep refrigerated (10).
- Considered extremely safe, even in pregnancy and nursing; possible side effects: headaches, heartburn, nausea, or insomnia; there are no drug-interactions (12).

The German Commission E Monographs put rose hip information in a chapter called "Unapproved Herbs" and separates information on three aspects of a hip: the rose hip, the rose hip and seed, and the rose hip seed. To summarize: they list the composition of each, i.e.; "Rose hip consists of the ripe, fresh or dried seed receptacle of various spp. of the genus Rosa, freed from seed and attached trichomes as well as preparations thereof"; they list the medicinal uses for each, and then, they say: "Activity in most of the aforementioned indications have not been substantiated, activity in treating or preventing possible vitamin C deficiency is questionable in view of the herb's low vitamin C content that rapidly declines with storage." There are "no known risks" and the evaluation is:

"Since effectiveness for some claims are not sufficiently documented and for others not at all, therapeutic application is not recommended, if only consumption of preparations as a vitamin C- containing food is primarily assigned to the food industry. There is no objection to its use as a taste enhancer in tea mixtures." (3)

Rose Hips as Used by Native Americans

OF THE 20 roses listed in *Native American Ethnobotany*, rose hips of 14 species were used much as we do now, yet there are some interesting observations. Eaten fresh, dried, cooked and roasted, and sometimes only as starvation food.

- Juice extracted, boiled, mixed with other juices.
- Frozen (in Alaska) and stored for future use.
- Made into jams, jellies, pies and puddings.
- Hips mixed with dried salmon eggs to enhance flavor.
- Crushed hips used to make pemmican.
- Firm hips made into beads, often to be worn by children.
- Medicinal teas for coughs, sore, itchy throats, especially for babies.
- Fruit skin is eaten for stomach troubles.
- Decoction is drunk for rheumatism, colds, sore throats, fevers, indigestion, kidney ailments, as a wash for skin sores and scabs.
- Hips chewed by women in labor to hasten delivery.
- Hips are commonly foraged by coyotes and bears (the latter before hibernation) (11).

Some Questions and Rose Hip Research

ALL OF THE information transmitted in this article is from books, magazines and newsletters, purchased, subscribed to, and/or read in a library or online. My intention was to survey many sources available to me and choose what I thought was common knowledge as well as some recent information. In this way I hoped to help clear up some questions I had and share some answers with readers who may have had the same wonderings, for instance:

Rose hips are fruits, aren't they? Yes, when they contain the seeds; when they don't, they are considered false fruits, receptacles, hypanthia or just rose hips.

What do you mean roses have prickles, not thorns; all my life those thorns have prickled me! Prickles are epidermal, thorns are more than epidermal.

What about those bristly hairs inside the rose hip seed cavity; they remind me of the choke in artichoke? It's good to scrape them out with the seeds, also called matured ovules, achene-type fruits, or achenes, if you can. Otherwise, I guess they get filtered out or pulverized in processing.

Is the vitamin C in rose hips equivalent to that of oranges? Hard to say: how many rose hips per how many oranges... think of the stories we've heard or read over the years about how rose hip preparations have presumably helped many people with limited access to citrus fruits (7).

Can it be harmful to use rose hips/rose hip preparations as tea and food supplements? No, even though they are not considered an "approved herb" because of the questionable levels of vitamin C and rapidly declining C content during storage, no risks are known, consumption is primarily assigned to the food industry, and there is no objection to their use as a flavor enhancer in tea mixtures.

How did First Nation peoples on this continent use rose hips? Much the same way as do we Afro-Indo-European descendants, without modern conveniences.

Should I stop taking drug store or co-op vitamin C in powder, tablet or capsule forms and change to rose hips/rose hip preparations? Read up on it; and consult with your health-care practitioner. Rose hip vitamin C is usually supplemented with the synthetic (8).

Bibliography

1. Albert-Matesz, Rachel. "Hip, Hip, Hooray for the Taste of Rose Hips – Cherry Red Seedpods That Add Taste and Nutrition to So Many Foods." *The Herb Companion*, Feb/Mar. 2000, pp.36-39.

2. Bagust, Harold. *The Gardener's Dictionary of Horticultural Terms*. New York: Sterling, 1992.

3. Blumenthal, Mark, Senior Ed. with Busse, Goldberg, Gruenwald, Hall, Klein, Riggins & Rister. *The Complete German Commission E Monographs – Therapeutic Guide to Herbal Medicines*. Austin, Texas: The American Botanical Council in co-operation with Integrative Medicine Communications, Boston, Massachusetts, 1998, pp.368-369.

4. Burnie, David. *PLANT–Discover the Fascinating World of Plants–Their Structure, Variety, and Life History*. London: Doring Kindersley, 2000, pp.26-27.

5. Capon, Brian. *Botany For Gardeners – An Introduction & Guide*. Portland, Oregon: Timber Press, 1990, pp. 46, 74, 88, Glossary.

6. Facciola, Stephen. *CORNCUCOPIA II – A Source Book of Edible Plants*. Vista, California: Kampong Publications, 1998, pp. 206-208.

7. Gail, Peter A. "On the Trail of the Volunteer Vegetable – Clinging Fruits of Winter – Part 2 Rose Hips". *The Bu$iness of Herbs*, March/April 1998, pp.18-19.

8. Leung, Albert Y. and Steven Foster. *Encyclopedia of Common Natural Ingredients Used in Food, Drugs, and Cosmetics*. New York: John Wiley & Sons, Inc., 1996, pp. 443-444.

9. Meletis, Chris D. "Complete Guide to Safe Herbs". *Doring Kindersley Natural Health Magazine*, first American edition, London, 2002, p. 50.

10. Moerman, Daniel E. *Native American Ethnobotany*. Portland, Oregon: Timber Press, 1998, pp. 482-486.

11. Mountain Rose Herbs catalog, Eugene, Oregon, 2011, p.46.

12. Stein, Diane. *Healing Herbs A to Z*. Berkeley, California: Crossing Press, 2009, p. 183.

13. Tucker, Arthur O. and Thomas DeBaggio. *The Encyclopedia of Herbs – A Comprehensive Reference to Herbs of Flavor and Fragrance*. Portland, Oregon: Timber Press, 2009, pp. 416, 418, 419.

14. Wikipedia Web site

15. Zomlefer, Wendy B. *Guide to Flowering Plant Families*. Chapel Hill, North Carolina: University of North Carolina Press, 1994, pp., 181-184, 368, 387, Glossary.

Harvest hips when they are a mature red.

Rose hips are packed full of vitamin C.

Pat Kenny began drawing and painting flowers with watercolors at the age of ten, continued studies in art and biology through college and the masters program in Medical and Biological Illustration at Johns Hopkins School of Medicine. In her 30 years at the National Institutes of Health, and in the Herb Society of America as well, Pat has contributed illustrations to a variety of publications. Inspired by The National Herb Garden, she has been gardening, cultivating herbs and giving slide-illustrated herb talks to county recreation classes, garden clubs, senior centers, and master gardener trainings for 30 years. Pat is now devoted to helping garden a Potomac Unit, H.S.A., Salvia Collection at Willow Pond Herbs in Fairfield, Pennsylvania. She enjoyed a two-year internship at The Green Farmacy Garden in Fulton, Maryland, goes back when she can, promotes food as medicine, and selectively gives programs about herbal plants in general.

Grandma's Little Rose

Skye Suter

I LEFT THE research and pencil biting to others and instead would like to share a few memories with you all—triggered by one little rosebush. Many years ago when I was starting my voyage into suburban gardening I was gifted a plant from my mother, which brings me many happy memories and good vibes whenever I am out in the garden. Like most moms, mine often comes bearing gifts when visiting her children. Mom is a plant lady and she frequently includes a plant among her other gifts. One day she showed up with a rosebush start, the scion from a bush originally growing in my grandparent's upstate New York yard. Mom had long since moved from there, but had transplanted a piece into her yard many years before eventually passing a cutting on to me.

So grandma's little rosebush that is neither particularly elegant nor showy is one of my favorite plants in the yard. It is a compact rosebush, probably of the miniature variety that sports a tiny, pinkish-red rose. It is my memory plant, bringing back thoughts of a childhood growing up in a small upstate New York town.

The most interesting things—a smell, a taste, a tactile touch or a visual object—trigger memories. When I see that rosebush, it makes me appreciative of the physical senses and my relationships with herbs and other plants. Running across the scent of lily-of-the-valley or lilac also triggers memories of Grandma, as well as a physical euphoria.

Time spent (or misspent) at my grandparent's house made for a bundle of good memories. While we were busy as children weeding, planting, picking or performing other garden chores, just being in the garden gave us endless memories to absorb and recall years later. I do remember the rosebush; it was planted along the side of the house in a planting bed and never made any particular impression on me at the time except that I did not like trimming it because of the prickles.

Grandma's rose gives me a good chuckle sometimes when I think of my childhood. Now when I am gardening in my yard and am working near the rosebush I smile and tell it thank you for helping me to remember. It smiles back at me and says, "You're welcome."

Skye Suter grows roses and herbs in her garden and illustrates them too. She is the owner of an oil painting depicting roses passed down to her through her grandmother. This painting now holds a place of honor in Skye's living room. She worked as an editorial art director and garden columnist at a newspaper. She also worked at a botanical garden and a non-profit promotional organization. Currently she is a food correspondent promoting the use of herbs in the kitchen. She is president of the Staten Island Herb Society and recently started a blog—www.skyesherbalburbles.com.

Remembering Roses

Betsy Williams

A NUMBER OF years ago, a friend was writing a book about roses and asked if I would be willing to contribute to it. My first reaction was no. I'm not a rosarian, I specialize in herbs. Herbs, their stories and uses, fill my life and bookshelves, not roses. I knew roses were often included in herb gardens for their fragrance and symbolism, but I didn't grow many of them. I certainly didn't feel expert enough to write about them. I would have to decline. Then, as I went about my day, rose memories began to creep out of hiding. By the end of the day my head was full of them. Roses had played an important part in my life. I just hadn't noticed.

Even though my father and favorite uncle were highly skilled gardeners and I have vivid memories of their gardens from my most distant childhood, my earliest rose memories date from 1946, the summer I turned seven. We were living in Washington, D.C. The war was over and so was my parents' marriage. My mother bought a house on Nantucket, an island 30 miles off the Massachusetts coast. Here, she told us, we would make a new home.

Nantucket was not rich and famous in 1946. It was a fishing community with a stable population of about 3,000 people that swelled considerably during July and August, when the summer people came for vacation. We would not be summer people; we were going be year-rounders.

We arrived in June and moved into an 1850s Greek Revival on the corner of Lily and North Liberty Streets. The house sat right on the edge of the street. A short, crushed scallop-shell driveway led to a two-story barn that filled the back of the property. There were two climbing trees, one on each side of the house and there were roses, lots of them. Huge tangled masses of small fragrant roses climbed weathered trellises nailed to the front and driveway sides of the house. A thicket of white cluster roses with sweet yellow honeysuckle twisting through it scrambled up the front of the house. The vine-filled canes arched over the front door, reaching for the second floor windows. Sprays of dainty pink roses, equally fragrant, blanketed the tall trellis on the driveway side.

I loved sipping the honeysuckle and burying my nose deep in the rose clusters to inhale as much of the delicious scent as possible. I have no memory of ever picking those roses or using them in any way, but their color, shape and fragrance mingled with the scent of honeysuckle are forever a part of me.

Nantucket exploded with roses in June—rambling roses, beach roses and even a few formal gardens of modern tea roses. Siasconset, a tiny fisherman's village invaded by Bohemian artists and actors from New York City in the 1890s, was always filled with visitors admiring its tiny, quaint cottages blanketed with rambling roses. The dunes bordering the island's beaches were covered with wild rose bushes that bloomed pink and fragrant and, by the end of summer, had red fruits resembling small tomatoes. Somehow we children knew those tomato look-alikes were edible, but we didn't dare try them. Our school art teacher hiked his students to the town beach each June to paint the roses. Our Girl Scout leaders did the same.

Many of the privet hedges on the island went untrimmed, so on warm June days the delicious scent of the creamy privet blossoms blended with the rose and honeysuckle fragrance. I remember riding my bike along Cliff Road and suddenly entering a pool of fragrant air. I stopped and just stood there, breathing. It was wonderful!

The house across the street from us was owned by summer people. It had a side yard enclosed with a Nantucket-style capped picket fence. Just inside the fence was a perennial border—a flower bed to me. It was the only one I remember ever seeing. The summer lady grew big golden-yellow roses. Nantucket roses were pink or white or red. I thought those yellow roses were splendid. I would hang over the fence to look at them. No one ever gave me one.

We left Nantucket in 1953 and moved to a farming community in southern Ohio. Roses and their fragrance disappeared from my life, replaced by corn, hogs and puberty.

Roses reentered my life briefly on my wedding day. I was in such a daze on that day that I never looked at the flowers that were thrust into my shaking hands. When I was told to, I dutifully flung the bouquet over my shoulder and left for my new life. Ten years later, when I attended florist school, I remembered my wedding flowers. I had to look at the wedding pictures to see what I was carrying—it was a bouquet of white roses.

Herbs took over my life in 1971. I researched, grew and retailed them. Roses returned as a symbolic, story-filled, fragrant herb. As the herb and dried flower business grew so did my involvement with roses. My staff and I were among the first to experiment with air drying fresh roses. We designed, wholesaled and retailed many products featuring roses: rose wreaths, rose pomanders, rose necklaces, rose hearts, rose topiaries, wedding herbs and friendship herbs.

The subject of the first article I ever sold was about a churchyard rose garden in Boston's North End. Created by a Franciscan priest, the garden, dedicated to world peace, showcased beautiful Peace roses.

Today, a variety of roses grow in my gardens— pink rugosas, an ancient eglantine, Victorian moss, the white rose of York and a Chinese-red apothecary. Tough little miniatures bloom all summer around a statue of St. Elizabeth of Hungary holding her apron full of roses. My favorite, fiercely defended each spring from the resident pruner, is a vigorous, fragrant climber that runs unchecked through one of our old apple trees. In June, when its creamy clusters cascade out of the tree and its rosy fragrance drifts through the garden, I'm momentarily seven years old again, back on Nantucket, smelling roses.

Betsy Williams has been growing, selling, decorating and teaching about living with herbs and flowers since 1972. Trained as a florist in Boston and England, she combines her floral and gardening skills with an extensive knowledge of history, plant lore and seasonal celebrations. A founding member of the International Herb Association, she served on its governing board for six years. In 1995 she was given the International Herb Association award for "her outstanding contributions to the herb industry."

The author of books and articles about herbs and flowers, she is a speaker and teacher at garden clubs, horticultural conferences, herb festivals and botanical gardens throughout the United States. Web site: www.BetsyWilliams.com E-mail: Betsy@betsywilliams.com

Recipes: The Kitchen

Rose Syrup is easily prepared using fresh or dried petals.

Pat Kenny makes floral ice cubes by dropping a rose petal
into each section of an ice cube tray and adding water.

Roses in the Kitchen

Susan Belsinger

WHEN USING ROSES for culinary purposes, it is important to smell and taste each type of rose, since some can be bland and mild-tasting while others can be bitter and sour. Usually if they have a strong scent, they have a similar taste of that fragrance, and generally, the more fragrant, the more flavor.

Color and bloom time of these perennial shrubs varies according to variety. These bushes range from one-foot miniatures to climbers that can grow up to twenty feet in height. The diversity in perfume can vary from no aroma at all to overwhelming fragrance. Older rose varieties (*Rosa* species) seem to have more fragrance than the newer hybrids. A few good choices that I like for edible flowers are *Rosa rugosa, R. damascena, R. x alba,* and *R. eglantine.*

For cooking, I prefer organic roses; only use blooms which have not been sprayed with pesticides or fungicides. To prepare roses for kitchen use, rinse them and shake the water from them. Turn the bloom over grasping the open flower in one hand, so that the stem is facing up. Use a sharp pair of scissors and snip right above the stem, and the petals will fall freely. Taste each rose—many roses have a bitter white part at the base of each petal—which should be snipped away. This can easily be done when removing petals all at once.

Rose petals are used in making rose water and syrup, to flavor alcohol and honey, jelly, butter, vinegar, rice puddings, custards, baklava, tea cakes, scones, cookies, frosting, ice cream and other desserts. They are ideal for crystallizing and are good macerated with wine and fruit. Rose water is popular in the cuisines of Eastern Europe, the Mid-East and North Africa and is used in pastries, cakes and sweets, often paired with nutmeats and/or dried fruits. If purchasing rose water, be sure that it is food grade and not used for perfumery. Some have rose oil added, so potency varies; be sure to taste and use sparingly—you can always add more—you don't want to overwhelm a dish.

Where savories are concerned, rose water and petals are often used in rice and couscous dishes, with vegetables, and with fowl and meat preparations, especially chicken. Dried petals are also combined with spices and herbs in blends like *ras-el-hanout* and *advieh* to season stews, *tagines* and grains. Together and separately, fresh petals and rose water are used to flavor sauces and vinaigrettes. Two of my favorite Moroccan-inspired salads are prepared with rose water: one is with grated carrots and the other uses sliced oranges and dates. Petals are most often used as a last-minute garnish for both savory and sweet dishes.

Simple Rose Water Syrup

THIS SYRUP IS an essential in most Mid-Eastern and Mid-Eastern Mediterranean kitchens. Each cook has their own way of preparing the syrup, so there are many variations of this classic ingredient. Basically, it is a syrup made from sugar and water to which rose water is added; sometimes additional ingredients like citrus juice or perhaps a spice like cinnamon is used. Adding the citrus, cuts the intensity of the rose perfume a bit and gives the syrup a different dimension. Choose a good-quality rose water—available at Mediterranean and Mid-Eastern markets and health food stores. My favorites are a Bulgarian one from Alteya Organics, which has to be ordered online or Cortas which is found commercially in many markets.

My recipe is an adaptation of my friend and colleague, Najmieh Batmangli (expert cook of Persian and Iranian cuisines), author of *New Food of Life: A Book of Ancient Persian and Modern Iranian Cooking and Ceremonies*, Mage Publishers, 1992. Najmieh makes a beverage from her rose water syrup using one part syrup to three parts water and serves it over two ice cubes. I like it with sparkling water, added to lemonade or champagne and other libations and used in ice cream, sorbets, puddings, with yogurt, compotes and pastries prepared with dried fruit and nuts, fruit salads, and desserts of all types.

Makes about 3 cups

1 cup water
3 cups sugar
About 2 tablespoons lemon or lime juice
1 teaspoon of zest, optional
1/3 to 1/2 cup rose water

In a saucepan, combine the water and sugar and bring to a boil over medium-high heat. Reduce heat to medium and simmer for 5 minutes. Add the citrus juice, zest if using it and the rose water, stirring, and let simmer about 10 minutes. This makes a standard, not-too-thick syrup. If a thicker syrup is desired, reduce it down further, stirring occasionally.

Remove from heat and allow to come to room temperature. Strain and pour into a clean canning jar or bottle, seal and label. Store in the refrigerator.

Chocolate Rose-Scented Soufflé

ORIGINALLY I TRIED preparing this recipe with rose water, but the flavor was not strong enough. Rose syrup is good in this recipe, however cooking down fresh organic rose petals takes longer, so I use the easy recipe (above) for this dessert. This quintessential syrup is used in many desserts and dishes in Mid-Eastern cuisine and surrounding regions. It marries well with chocolate for this unique soufflé.

Serves 6 to 8

1/2 cup half-and-half cream
4 ounces semisweet chocolate, broken into pieces
1 ounce unsweetened chocolate, broken into pieces
1/4 cup sugar
2 pinches salt
5 extra-large eggs, separated
1/4 cup rose syrup
Whipping cream
Organic rose petals or candied rose petals

Preheat the oven to 375 º F. Generously butter six 1-cup ramekins or custard cups and sprinkle lightly with sugar.

Combine the cream, chocolate, sugar, and salt in a heavy-bottomed saucepan. Place over medium low heat. Whisk the chocolate as it melts to make a smooth mixture. Remove from heat when the chocolate is completely melted.

Beat the 5 yolks, one at a time, into the chocolate mixture. Whisk the rose geranium syrup into the chocolate, 1 tablespoon at a time. In a separate bowl, beat the egg whites until stiff but not dry.

Whisk about a cup of the egg whites into the chocolate mixture. Then pour the chocolate mixture into the whites and fold until just blended. Pour the mixture into the prepared dishes and bake in the lower half of the oven for 12 minutes, until they are set.

While the soufflés are cooking, whip about ½ cup whipping cream with 1 tablespoon of sugar until almost stiff. Whisk in about 1 tablespoon rose syrup and taste; add a little more if desired.

Remove the soufflés from the oven. Scatter a few fresh rose petals or rose geranium flowers over the soufflés if you have them, or garnish each soufflé with a candied rose petal. Serve the soufflés immediately and pass the whipping cream. (You have about 5 to 7 minutes to serve the soufflés before they start to deflate.)

If you have leftover soufflés, you can refrigerate them and eat them the next day. Their texture will be more dense, but they are still tasty served at cool room temperature.

Drop Scones with Rose Petals and Pistachios

THESE SCONES ARE a bit more exotic than your everyday scone and they are drizzled with a rose icing. The latter is optional—if you prefer to serve them in a more traditional manner—pass a very lightly whipped cream and rose petal jelly as accompaniments. This recipe is from *Flowers in the Kitchen* by Susan Belsinger, Interweave Press, 1996.

Makes about 2 dozen scones

2 1/4 cups unbleached white flour
2 teaspoons sugar
3/4 teaspoon salt
2 teaspoons baking powder
1/2 teaspoon baking soda
2 to 3 pinches cinnamon
4 tablespoons unsalted butter
1/3 cup shelled pistachios, lightly toasted, and coarsely ground
1 cup cream
1 teaspoon rose water
A good handful of rose petals
1 cup confectioners' sugar
1 tablespoon rose jelly or 1 tablespoon red currant jelly mixed with about 1/2 teaspoon rose water
2 to 3 teaspoons water

Preheat oven to 425 °F. Combine the dry ingredients in a large bowl and blend thoroughly. Cut in the butter until the mixture resembles a coarse meal. Stir in the pistachios.

Stir the cream together with the rose water. Rinse the rose petals and pat them dry. Cut them into a *chiffonade*; there should be about 2 tablespoons. Stir them into the cream and add the liquid to the dry ingredients and stir to form a soft dough. Drop the dough by the heaping tablespoonful onto an ungreased baking sheet. Bake the scones for 10 to 12 minutes or until golden brown. Prepare the icing while the scones are baking.

Combine the confectioners' sugar, jelly, and 2 teaspoons water in a small bowl and whisk until smooth. Add another teaspoon water if icing seems too thick—it will melt a little if the scones are warm.

Remove the scones to a baking rack to cool slightly before drizzling them with icing. They are best served warm, right after baking.

If you want to prepare them in advance, cool them completely without icing and store them in an air-tight container. Wrap them in foil and gently reheat in a 325° F oven for about 10 to 15 minutes. Drizzle the icing over them while they are warm.

"We bring roses, beautiful fresh roses,
Dewy as the morning and coloured like the dawn;
Little tents of odour, where the bee reposes,
Swooning in sweetness of the bed he dreams upon."

Thomas Buchanan Read, The New Pastoral, Book VII, line 51.

Susan Belsinger loves immersing herself in all things herbal and looks forward with gusto to researching, growing, cooking, and photographing each new Herb of the Year™. Growing vegetables, herbs, and flowers organically, harvesting them at their peak, and bringing them into the kitchen to create healthy recipes is a way of life for Susan. She is passionate about herbs and her work—sharing the joy of gardening and cooking through teaching and writing—and inspiring others to get in touch with their senses of smell and taste.
www.susanbelsinger.com

Flavor and Fragrance of Roses

Karen England

> "I haven't any modesty when it comes to my old roses.
> They're heavenly."
>
> ---Tasha Tudor

WHEN I WAS a child my father read to me at night before bed and the books he read were titles like the *Chronicles of Narnia* by C.S. Lewis and *The Wind in the Willows* by Kenneth Grahame. It is not surprising then that the foods, places and plants, among other things, that appear in the books that Dad read impacted me as I grew up.

It is Kenneth Grahame's breathtaking writing, like this quote from his classic book first published in 1908, *The Wind in the Willows*, (where Mole and Ratty are in a row boat on the water) that worked its literary magic on my psyche and compelled me as a child and, now as an adult, to notice the beauty of nature:

"On either side of them, as they glided onwards, the rich meadow-grass seemed that morning of a freshness and a greenness unsurpassable. Never had they noticed the roses so vivid, the willow-herb so riotous, the meadow-sweet so odorous and pervading."

These books of my childhood affected me so much so, that when I traveled during my senior year of high school with my A.P. English class to London and Stratford in England (long before my name would become England) on a theater tour, I made a point of visiting the sites and eating the foods made famous by the literature of my childhood and the authors I loved.

I was especially anxious to try "Turkish Delight"—the confection that was Edmund Pevensie's downfall in Lewis' *The Lion, the Witch and the Wardrobe*. It was during that trip as a teenager that I learned roses were edible, long before I ever embraced herbs as a way of life, because I found out they were the candy's major flavoring. Up until that time roses to me were merely just cut flowers in bouquets and merchandise sold in my family's plant nursery where I worked after school.

Fast-forward ten years later and I am still employed at the same family nursery business and this time I traveled on vacation to New England for the first time (this trip was also before I became an England!). During that trip, on a glorious day in early July, I visited the Hancock Shaker Village in Pittsfield, Massachusetts. As we drove into the village I saw the many roses that lined the roads of the community, were all still in bloom. The roses, I would learn later, were grown specifically to make rose water and harvest rose hips "for sale, domestic use and the infirmary" just as they did in the early 1800s.

According to Rita Buchanan in *The Shaker Herb And Garden Book,* circa 1996, while speaking of the Shakers working in the middle decades of the nineteenth century, "They grew two kinds of roses, and it is not always clear which kind is being referred to in journal entries or catalog listings. Both have dark pink or crimson flowers that are very fragrant, and both can be used for making rose water and rose oil and for drying." Everyone now agrees that the two varieties used were the damask rose and the apothecary rose.

In the mid-1800s, one sister of the New Lebanon Shaker Community said, "a rose was useful, not ornamental–its mission was to be made into rose-water–to be sold and to… flavor apple pies." Shaker rose water and rose hips are still produced in the same manner as of old and are available to this day from the few remaining Shakers of Sabbathday Lake, New Gloucester, Maine (online at www.shaker.lib.me.us/catalog.html). I have purchased these and other items from their online herb catalog and, if you decide not to make your own waters and teas from your own grown roses like the articles in this book encourage, then I highly recommend their products.

Still another ten years after that trip (I am now married and named England) my husband and I planted 70-some old and modern roses when designing the edible herb gardens and landscapes at our current home. Not all those roses, chosen mainly for their catalog descriptions that said they were very fragrant, turned out to be good choices. However, most of our choices were great and have been providing me with delicious blossoms and healthy hips for almost a dozen years.

Some of our roses have died over the years—most notably 'Mister Lincoln' which died very early in our garden's history. I named the gopher that ate this rose—you guessed it: John Wilkes Booth! Other roses were unhappy, never thriving, so we yanked those out and we probably have 60 plants remaining (although I haven't actually counted).

'Scentimental' is a favorite for its striped appearance.

Here is an incomplete list—just our favorites—of the roses currently growing at our home and business, which we call Edgehill Herb Farm; (except where noted we planted only one of each).

'Aloha'
'Berries and Cream'
'Cecile Brunner'
'Double Delight' (planted 2 of these for obvious reasons)
'Eden'
'Fourth of July'
'Gertrude Jekyll'
'Heart of Gold'
'High Hopes'
'Joseph's Coat'
'La Reine Victoria'
Rosa californica (The native California rose; this is my replacement for the Apothecary rose which up and died early on.)
'Scentimental'
'Shadow Dancer'
'Souvenir de la Malmaison'
'The Herbalist' (Planted 2 in case one died, which did not happen so I have them flanking both sides of the soap shop entrance, so apropos!)
'Yellow Rose of Texas' (Not!—it is yellow but probably mismarked and not the rose I thought.)

In caring for rose bushes it is best to always remember two main things:

1. *They are water hogs and will drink all the water you give.* However, if you judiciously water roses they can and will adjust to the amount given and become almost drought tolerant. I think a little less water rather than too much makes the rose fragrance and flavor more intense, which is a good thing for both.

2. *Roses are easy to grow.* However, if you want to show roses, something I do not want to do, then this advice does not apply. I have friends who are national, award-winning Rosarians and they have—this is no joke—refrigerators installed in their garden shed which is out in the midst of their backyard rose fields! Yes, I said fields. Each day leading up to a rose show they cut flowers, mark each with a

tag containing vital info: name, date, etc., and put the cut roses into the garden fridge. Their shed also has volumes of record-keeping books. This does not sound like a fun way to garden to me! Once the day of the rose show rolls around, they go into the fridge and select the best roses of the week's crop to take to the show. They employ full time gardeners who fertilize and water and prune the roses constantly. To my mind all this requires way too much work!

I'm convinced that it is the professional rose-showing competitors like my friends, as well as advertising campaigns of fertilizer, pesticide and fungicide companies that gives the whole world the idea that roses are hard to grow. They are not. Roses are very forgiving and I just water mine some, prune them a little and fertilize organically occasionally. Oh, and I eat them a lot! Since roses grow on every continent in the world and have since the beginning of time it is obvious to me they can't be that hard to grow. My Rosarian friends are always scandalized when I serve them roses to eat that they would have entered into a competition. I tell them that I would only be scandalized if they tried to kill me by serving me their roses as food…

Speaking of food… here are some terrific rose recipes from my collection.

Sweet Rose Gin and Tonic

WHEN I WAS 17 and traveling in Great Britain with my classmates I did not drink alcohol and one of my friends kindly introduced me to a drink called "Tonic and Bitters" so I could order something "British" at the pubs and bars that was alcohol free. I still order it to this day even though I now also drink alcohol. I developed this "Sweet Rose G & T" recipe to add gin to my go-to drink. It accentuates the rose ingredient that Hendrick's Gin from Scotland is known for.

Makes 1 drink

Cracked ice
2-ounces Hendrick's ® Gin, or your favorite gin
Juice of 1/2 a lime

2 teaspoons rose-infused simple syrup or *Freezer Rose Petal Jam* (see below)

1/2 teaspoon Peychaud's ® or Angostura Bitters ® (Peychaud's makes the drink more pink than Angostura—and more anise-flavored)

Tonic Water

Fresh rose with stem for swizzle stick, thorns removed

Fill a cocktail shaker with cracked ice and add the gin, lime juice, rose simple syrup or jam, and bitters. Top off with tonic water.

Shake and strain into a chilled glass and garnish with a rose.

Karen's Sweet Rose Gin and Tonic

I HAVE FOUND at least three versions of this recipe over the years, all of which I believe to have their beginnings in a recipe called "Uncooked Rose Petal Jam" from Euell Gibbons classic book *Stalking the Healthful Herbs*, 1966. However, the version I love most comes from retired rose enthusiast, Gerry Krueger's self-published cookbook *Everything's Coming Up Roses*, circa 2000. Before she retired and closed her "Blossoms and Bloomers" business and Web site in Spokane, Washington, this recipe was available for free online and I reprint it here with confidence. I have adapted it slightly. It is truly delicious, wonderfully beautiful and easy.

Note: Gerry insists you must remove the white portion at the base of each petal that is said to be bitter, but I do not do this and I still have delicious jam.

Makes approximately 1 quart

2 cups packed fragrant rose petals, pesticide free, of course! (reds and pinks are best, avoid white, which tends to turn brown)
About 1 teaspoon zest from an unwaxed lemon, optional
1 cup apple juice
4 cups of superfine or ultrafine sugar, sometimes sold as "Baker's Sugar".
(I have had a problem with regular granulated sugar dissolving in this recipe and confectioners' sugar is too fine.)
3-ounce pouch liquid fruit pectin, such as Certo® brand
1/4 cup fresh lemon juice

Combine the cleaned rose petals, lemon zest, if using, and apple juice in a blender and pulse to very finely mince the petals. Put the sugar in a large bowl and pour the minced roses and apple juice over the sugar. Stir often to dissolve the sugar for a period of about 20 to 30 minutes.

Meanwhile, empty the contents of the liquid pectin pouch into a small bowl and stir in the lemon juice. When the sugar is dissolved, stir the pectin mixture into the sugar and petal mixture and blend well making sure the sugar is no longer grainy. Pour into clean, freezer-safe containers and label. Let stand at room temperature for 24 hours to set. For

Easy-to-make and have on hand: Rose Petal Freezer Jam

This Amb-ROSE-ia is a rosy version of the fruit salad known as Ambrosia.

immediate use, store in the refrigerator for 3 weeks or freeze up to a year.

Use this jam in recipes for everything from baked goods to adult beverages or just slather on scones and serve with tea.

Amb-ROSE-ia

HERE IS MY modern take on an old-fashioned fruit salad. I use all organic ingredients in this but, of course, you can make this with the ingredients you have as long as the roses are free of pesticides and fungicides.

Tip: If you insist on clipping off the white central tip of each petal, which is said to be bitter, do so by holding the whole rose blossom in one hand, twist out the stem and cut off all the white all at once with kitchen shears. However, you should know I never bother with this…

Serves 4

1 handful unsweetened dried coconut
1 handful dried tart cherries
2 fragrant red or pink roses, petals only
8-ounce can pineapple chunks in 100% juice, separate juice from chunks and reserve
1 banana, peeled and sliced
1 'Honey Mandarin' orange or similar citrus, peeled and sectioned

In a medium serving bowl, soak the coconut, cherries and rose petals in the pineapple juice and chill for an hour or more (or less—for as long as you have). After the soaking time, put the pineapple chunks, mandarin and banana in with the juice, cherries, roses and coconut.

I like to put the juice in the serving bowl and then add the coconut, cherries and rose petals. Then I top with the pineapple and mandarin but I don't mix the layers. I cover and chill. Later when I am going to serve I add the banana and stir. Stir and chill.

Serve with a dollop of yogurt.

Jo Seagar's Rose Turkish Delight

THIS RECIPE IS reprinted with permission from *The Cook School Recipes*, Jo Seagar, Random House, New Zealand, 2008.

This centuries-old rosewater candy is also known as "Lokum" and once I tasted it in London in 1977, I never looked at a rose the same again. Research has shown me that the original rosewater Lokum candy known as Turkish Delight did not contain gelatin, which is a common ingredient in most modern recipes. However, New Zealander Jo Seagar's version does not and that not only makes this confection more like the original, but also perfect for vegans and vegetarians. My college roommate and BFF remembers her Michigan grandmother making a version of Turkish Delight every Christmas to give and to serve. It was the favorite item in the care packages she sent to us in California.

Makes 60 pieces

4 cups sugar
4 1/2 cups boiling water
1 tablespoon citric acid (sour salt)
1 cup cornstarch, plus 2 tablespoons, divided
1 teaspoon cream of tartar
1 tablespoon culinary rose water, homemade or store-bought
1 to 2 drops pink food coloring, optional
3 tablespoons confectioners' sugar
Line a 20-cm x 20-cm (8- x 8-inch) square cake pan with tin foil and spray with baking spray.

Place sugar, 1 1/2 cups boiling water, and citric acid in a small heavy non-stick saucepan. Stir until the sugar dissolves and bring the mixture to a boil.

Boil gently, without stirring, just swirling the saucepan around occasionally until the mixture reaches the soft-ball stage (116° C/ 240° F).

Whisk the 1 cup of cornstarch, cream of tartar and remaining 3 cups of boiling water together in a medium-sized heavy non-stick saucepan.

Slowly add the sugar syrup to this mixture, whisking constantly to avoid lumps forming. Gently, while you continue stirring, bring to a simmer and cook for a further 30 to 40 minutes until it is pale golden in color and very thick. Stir in the rose water and food coloring (if using). Pour into prepared pan and cool, and then set in the fridge overnight.

Sift the confectioners' sugar and the remaining 2 tablespoons cornstarch together. Turn the *Turkish Delight* out of the pan and cut into 2 cm (approximately 1/2-inch) cubes. Roll in the sugar cornstarch mixture. Store in an air-tight container for up to 2 weeks. Separate the layers with sheets of wax paper or parchment.

Karen uses *Rosa californica* in place of the Apothecary rose.

Karen England clutching an armload of her homegrown roses.

Karen England still works as a consultant for her family's plant nursery, Sunshine Gardens, which is celebrating its 40th year in Encinitas, California. She is a popular presenter, giving garden talks and teaching herbal classes throughout Southern California. Karen also works from her home, located in the northern portion of San Diego County, as a freelance writer and crafter of soap and herbal sundries for her Web site www.edgehillherbfarm.com. She takes all her own garden and food photographs using an iPhone 3GS and often makes use of the phone's terrific Hipstamatic app.

Roses: My Memories and Recipes

Donna Frawley

WHEN I WAS a small child, living in Minnesota, I remember my father growing beautiful roses. They grew in a bed by themselves. It wasn't really a raised bed, but one that was mounded in the middle about 8-inches higher than it was around the edges. It was a rectangular bed with at least 24 beautiful roses growing in it! He would tend to them diligently. I think he used the time he cared for them as a way to relax from his high pressure job. I would watch him prune, trim, cultivate, feed and spray when necessary. When he originally prepared the bed he dug a two foot deep trench removing the old soil and replacing it with a mixture of good soil and manure. They thrived beautifully in this new home and we had roses blooming all summer long – hybrid teas and floribundas, mostly. They were his pride and joy. We moved from that home when I was eight, but I still have a vivid memory of all those beautiful roses.

My own personal experience with roses is different than my father's. I have a 'Belle Donna' damask rose (rather appropriately named if I might add). It is an old-fashioned rose. It was, at one time, growing in my grandmother's garden and she gave a start to my mother, who in turn gave a start to me. I moved it from our old house to our current location in 1989.

It is a vigorous rose with a habit of sending out underground branches, which send up new sprouts which increase the overall circumference of the base of the plant. To maintain a reasonable size, I remove some of these side shoots each year with a shovel. It requires no spraying or treatment of any kind. In the spring I just remove any dead wood and that is really all of the care that is required. In late June or early July it is full of dark pink buds opening up to a nice pink flower about 2½-inches

We have put a wire cage around the rose to help contain it as its thorns seem to jump out and grab passers-by.

This is one of the side shoots that will be removed; you can see the cage in the upper left, so this has overstepped its bounds.

across. It has a nice fragrance as well. I have harvested a lot of buds and dried them in a dehydrator to use on wreaths and other decorative items for my store. The ease in caring for this rose, its beautifully abundant, fragrant flowers, and the fact that it is from my grandmother's garden, makes this rose an all around winner in my book.

I have also grown miniature roses with success. Michigan winters can be a killer for standard roses, but miniatures seem to survive just fine. The three I have flower at some point each month, June, July and August. They aren't as prolific as the 'Belle Donna' but there are some flowers periodically throughout the summer which adds color to the garden where they are planted.

Green Salad with Herbs, Flowers and Sweet Creamy Rose Vinaigrette

THE FIRST TIME I had rose petals in a salad it was at the Montague Inn in Saginaw, Michigan. I was there giving a presentation on herbs out in their herb garden. When I finished my presentation all attendees would go inside for a wonderful herb luncheon. Their signature salad was the recipe that follows with some of my adaptations.

Serves 6 to 8

8 cups mixed greens, washed and dried
1/2 cup of your favorite fresh herbs, chopped (basil, fennel, marjoram, parsley, tarragon, etc.)
1 cup mixed, fresh, fragrant rose petals and dill flowers
Salt and pepper
3/4 cup dried cherries or dried cranberries
1/2 cup crumbled feta or blue cheese

In a large salad bowl combine the salad greens with the herbs and flowers, reserving a good handful of the flowers to garnish. Season with salt and pepper and scatter the dried cherries over the salad.

Toss lightly with the vinaigrette and sprinkle with desired cheese. Serve on individual plates and garnish with the reserved flowers. Serve with a slice of fruit bread.

Sweet Creamy Rose Vinaigrette

I LIKE USING opal basil vinegar because of the flavor and I want a pink dressing and the opal basil will add to that. If you don't have opal basil vinegar, you can use green basil, raspberry or tarragon vinegar. With the egg, Egg Beaters® work well because there is no worry of salmonella as with raw egg and it will keep longer (about 2 weeks) in the refrigerator where raw egg needs to be used within a week. The egg or Egg Beaters® are used as an emulsifier which holds the oil in suspension (it won't separate out).

Makes about 2 cups

3 tablespoons opal basil vinegar
1 to 2 teaspoons rose water
2 tablespoons honey
2 tablespoons dried cherries or dried cranberries
2 tablespoons fresh opal basil
2 tablespoons fresh rose petals
1 cup olive oil
1 large egg OR 1/4 cup Egg Beaters®
2 to 3 tablespoons yogurt
Salt and pepper

Put vinegar, rose water, honey, dried fruit, opal basil and rose petals in food processor. Blend slightly to chop herbs and petals. Add egg and yogurt; season with salt and pepper and mix well. As food processor is running, slowly add oil in a steady stream. Blend well. It should be as thick as pudding. Add more vinegar and/or rose water if you want a more intense flavor. Pour on salad and lightly toss. Store in refrigerator for about 2 weeks (if Egg Beaters® are used).

I WANTED A cookie featuring roses for the 2011 IHA conference as our theme was "Roses and Other Herbs Around the World." My friend Laura LaLonde shared her Mary's Sugar Cookies recipe with me which was from her mother's *Betty Crocker Cookie Book*, 1963, submitted by Mary Herman. I adapted the original recipe with the addition of rose water and the glazes are my creations.

Makes about 5 dozen 2-to 2 1/2-inch cookies

1 1/2 cups sifted confectioners' sugar
1 cup salted butter, softened
1 egg large
1 teaspoon rose water
1 teaspoon pure vanilla extract
1/2 teaspoon almond extract
2 1/2 cups all-purpose flour
1 teaspoon baking soda
1 teaspoon cream of tartar

In the bowl of an electric mixer, mix sugar and butter together thoroughly. Add egg, rose water and extracts and mix thoroughly. Sift flour, baking soda and cream of tartar together and blend dry ingredients into butter mixture. Put dough in a bowl or flattened onto plastic wrap and seal and chill dough 2 to 3 hours.

Heat oven to 375° F. Divide dough in half and roll out each piece, one at a time, to 3/16-inch thick on a floured pastry cloth. Cut into desired shapes and place on lightly greased cookie sheets. Bake for 7 to 8 minutes, just until lightly golden. Transfer to cooling rack.

I MAKE SOME of the glaze just a bit thicker and pipe it around the edge of the cookie and I make some thinner to flood the cookie with a layer of glaze inside of the piping.

For thicker piping glaze:

2 cups confectioners' sugar, sifted
1 tablespoon rose water
3 drops red food coloring, optional
1 to 1 1/2 tablespoons milk or half-and-half

Put confectioners' sugar in a bowl. In a custard cup mix together the rose water, food coloring and milk or half-and-half and add to the bowl. Mix thoroughly with a fork, making sure it is thick enough to put in pastry bag and pipe around the edges of the cookies. Let dry slightly before flooding it with thinner glaze.

For thinner layering glaze:

2 cups confectioners' sugar, sifted
1 tablespoon rose water
3 drops red food coloring, optional
2 tablespoons milk or half-and-half

Put confectioners' sugar in a bowl. In a custard cup mix together the other ingredients and add to the bowl. Mix thoroughly. It should be thin enough to run off of a spoon.

Using a small teaspoon, dip into the mixture and put some glaze on each cookie and spread it with the back of the spoon. Add sprinkles if desired while glaze is still wet.

Let dry completely before putting in bag or in air-tight container. If stacking cookies make sure to put waxed paper or parchment between layers. They can be frozen after glaze dries and is totally set up, otherwise they will stick to one another.

When removing from the freezer, take them out of the container and put them on cooling racks because moisture will condense on top of cookies making the glaze sticky. Wait until cookies are dry and put in individual bags or an air-tight container layered with waxed paper or parchment.

Pretty in pink: Rose Butter Cookies with Rose Glaze
cut out with a flower-shaped cookie cutter.

Donna Frawley started her business, Frawley's Fine Herbary, in 1983 when a friend suggested she share some of her herbs and herbal knowledge with the community. She began by selling at the local Farmer's Market and that Fall opened a home-based business which continues today. Her Home Economics background helped her develop 57 of her own culinary herb mixes. She has authored three books, **The Herbal Breads Cookbook**, **Edible Flowers Book**, and **Our Favorite Recipe**s, and has a DVD **Cooking With Herbs**, and she also writes a monthly culinary herb column in her local newspaper and has contributed to the Herb Companion Magazine. She has spoken on a variety of culinary herb topics and has done cooking demonstration all over the country. She is a regular instructor at Whiting Forest where she has taught over 20 classes.

Donna is a member of the Valley Herb Society, the Great Lakes Herb Business Association, the Michigan Herb Associates and the International Herb Association (IHA). You can purchase Donna's delightful culinary mixes and read her blog on her Web site: www.frawleysfineherbary.com frawleyherbs@yahoo.com

An Ancient Flavor

Stephen Lee

THE HISTORICAL ART of enhancing foods with the flavors of flowers is most often associated with the cooking of Medieval times; however, flowers—particularly roses, have long been used in the kitchens of Middle-Eastern sultans and sheiks. These unique flavor boosters were most probably brought to the Mediterranean basin by Genghis Khan and/or other warring tribesmen from the east long before calendars were an everyday commodity.

Moroccan Tagine of Chicken, Squash and Roses

TAGINE IS BOTH the name of a conical cooking vessel traditionally used in North Africa and of the stew-like dish prepared in it. This recipe uses a more readily available Dutch oven; however, if you have a traditional tagine by all means use it. You will need to prepare the Moroccan-Style Spice Mixture below in order to make this dish.

NOTE: *Ensure that the rose petals you use in this dish are organic and chemical-free. The finished dish should not be perfumed with the scent of roses; the flower in this recipe is used as an accent and overall mellowing sweetener.*

Serves 6

2 pounds chicken pieces: breasts, thighs and legs
About 2 tablespoons *Moroccan-Style Spice Mixture* (see below)
3 tablespoons olive oil
2 large yellow onions, sliced thick lengthwise
8 cloves garlic, peeled and halved

6 threads saffron, crushed
3-pound butternut squash, peeled, seeded and cut into 1-inch cubes
1 1/2 cups chicken broth
1 cup golden raisins
1/2 cup dates, chopped small
3 tablespoons fresh rose petals, chopped coarse
About 4 tablespoons honey, for drizzling
1/2 cup Italian parsley, chopped

Lay the chicken pieces on a baking sheet, sprinkle about 1 tablespoon of the spice mixture over and rub well into each piece, cover gently and let sit on kitchen counter for 1 hour.

Place a 4-quart Dutch oven over medium heat, when hot add 2 tablespoons of the olive oil, swirl pan to coat bottom. Add chicken and cook, for about 8 minutes, turning to brown the meat evenly. Remove the chicken to a platter and reserve.

Add the remaining olive oil, then add the onions, garlic and saffron and cook, stirring well, for about 5 minutes. Add the butternut squash, sprinkle with 1 tablespoon of the remaining spice mixture and mix well to combine. Return the reserved chicken to the pot with the broth and bring to a boil. Reduce heat to low, cover and simmer very gently for 1 hour. Check after 20 minutes to make sure the tagine is not bubbling and is simmering slowly.

Add the raisins, dates and 2 tablespoons of the rose petals, cover and continue to cook, over low heat, until the chicken is done and the squash is tender, about 15 to 20 minutes more.

Remove chicken and squash to a warmed serving platter, spoon pan juices and fruits over, drizzle with honey and sprinkle with parsley and remaining rose petals. Serve with couscous or other pasta.

RAS EL HANOUT, a spice rub mixture now most generally associated with Morocco, is one that encompasses the traditional tastes of the southern Mediterranean basin. It is authentically made using ground rose or lavender petals along with a mixture of some twenty or more spices and herbs. Here, I offer you a quick and easy version of the famous spice blend, which is used in my recipe for the delicious chicken tagine above. You can use the blend on most any meat before roasting or grilling. I tried it on some salmon fillets recently and my guest just raved, so don't be afraid to be adventurous in your Middle-Eastern cookery.

Makes about 1/4 cup

1 tablespoon kosher salt
1 teaspoon red pepper flakes, crushed
1 teaspoon cardamom, ground
1 teaspoon cloves, ground
1 teaspoon turmeric, ground
1 teaspoon cinnamon, ground
1 teaspoon ginger, ground
1 teaspoon coriander, ground
1/2 teaspoon black pepper, freshly ground
2 teaspoons dried rose petals, ground fine

In a small bowl, combine all of the spices together, blending well. Spoon the mixture into a jar and label.

Herb and Rose-Stuffed Chicken Breasts

ENSURE THAT ROSES are food grade and have not been treated with chemicals. This beautiful and delicious entrée would make an elegant dish served atop your favorite recipe for Saffroned Rice.

Serves 8

1 tablespoon unsalted butter
1 medium yellow onion, chopped fine
10-ounce package frozen, chopped spinach, thawed and drained well
1 tablespoon fresh-chopped tarragon
2 tablespoons fresh-chopped chives
2 tablespoons fresh-chopped Italian parsley
1/4 cup fresh-chopped rose petals
1 teaspoon rose water
1/2 cup ricotta cheese
1/2 cup shredded, aged cheese, (Asiago, Parmesan, etc.)
Kosher salt
Freshly ground white pepper
8 large chicken breasts, boned with skin left on

Melt the butter in a large skillet over medium heat, when hot add the onions and cook until tender, about 5 minutes. Remove from heat and add the spinach, chopped herbs and rose petals, rose water, ricotta and aged cheeses and mix well. Season with kosher salt and pepper to taste.

Preheat oven to 350° F. Trim fat and loosen skin from each chicken breast and stuff 1/8 of the herb and cheese mixture under the skin. Tuck the skin and meat under the breast, forming a neat, rounded dome shape. Repeat with remaining breasts. Place the stuffed breasts in a well-greased baking sheet.

Bake prepared breasts in the preheated 350° F. oven for 30 minutes or until the skin is a nice golden brown. Serve hot from the oven. Garnish with additional fresh rose petals.

Savory Rose and Chive Cheesecake

ENSURE THAT ROSES are food grade and not treated with any chemicals. This recipe offers a great opportunity to use a colorful variety of rose petals, as the petal colors will really pop against the white cheesecake. Use smaller portions as an appetizer or cut larger slices for a nice summer luncheon.

Serves 10

Crust
4 slices dark rye bread, made into fine crumbs
4 tablespoons unsalted butter, melted

Lightly grease the sides and bottom of a 9-inch spring-form pan with solid shortening. Combine the butter and breadcrumbs in a small bowl. Transfer into the spring-form pan, spread evenly across the bottom and pat down gently to form the crust. Set aside.

Filling
15-ounce carton ricotta cheese, at room temperature
1/2 cup half-and-half, at room temperature
2 tablespoons flour, all-purpose
2 large eggs
1/3 cup fresh, full-scented rose petals, chopped small
3 tablespoons fresh-snipped chives
2 teaspoons rose water
1/4 teaspoon white pepper, freshly ground
1 teaspoon kosher salt

Preheat oven to 350° F.

Using a heavy-duty mixer combine the ricotta cheese, half-and-half and flour; blending until smooth. Add the eggs, one at a time, mixing well. Add the roses, chives, rose water, pepper and kosher salt and mix to blend thoroughly.

Pour the batter onto the prepared crust, spread evenly and put into the preheated 350° F oven and bake for 30 minutes, or until the center is just set. Remove from oven to a baking rack and cool to room temperature.

Serve slices plated or put the entire cheesecake onto a platter and serve as you would any like spread. Best served with unflavored crackers or dark rye bread.

Spinach in a Rose Garden

IT IS VERY important to ensure that all flowers used in cooking have been grown, harvested and stored without the use of pesticides and chemicals.

Serves 4

1 1/2 pounds fresh spinach, well-cleaned, trimmed and torn in small
   pieces
1 tablespoon rose water
2 tablespoons unsalted butter
2 tablespoons olive oil
1 tablespoon fresh rose petals, chopped
1 clove garlic, minced
1/4 cup currants
Kosher salt
Freshly ground white pepper

Place a heavy-bottomed pot over medium heat, when the pot is hot add the spinach and the rose water. Stir constantly and cook until the spinach is wilted. Remove from heat and reserve.

Heat a heavy medium-size skillet over medium heat, when hot add the butter and olive oil. When the oils are hot, but not smoking, add the roses and garlic and cook for 1 minute, stirring constantly. Add the reserved spinach, currants and season with kosher salt and pepper. Cook for 3 minutes more, serve immediately.

A NICE AND easy finish for the Moroccan Tagine or any meal is a simple dish of good vanilla ice cream. You can create a little herbal excitement by making a brittle to sprinkle over. Here is an easy recipe.

Makes brittle for 12 servings

1/2 cup oats, rolled, old-fashioned; not instant
2 teaspoons rose water
1 cup sugar

Put the oats into a heavy-bottomed 8-inch skillet and place over medium-low heat to toast lightly. Watch closely as they can burn easily. When the oats have a slightly toasty smell remove from heat and move around in the skillet to cool. Sprinkle the rose water over and with your hands mix the oats to ensure that the rose water has not formed clumps and that the oats have absorbed the rose water. Remove the oats to a bowl and reserve. Generously grease a small baking sheet and set aside.

Put the sugar in the skillet and place over medium heat until melted, shake the pan occasionally as the sugar melts. Reduce the heat to low; cook until the sugar is golden brown, stirring as needed.

Working quickly, stir the reserved toasted oats into the melted sugar and mix well. Pour the sugar and oat mixture onto the prepared baking sheet, spread to a thin layer as best you can. I put a piece of well-greased aluminum foil over the top, top that with a kitchen towel and press down with my hands to get a really thin brittle. If you use the aluminum foil—be sure to remove it immediately.

Allow the brittle to cool completely, break into large shards to use as a garnish on ice cream. Or just crush up the brittle completely and simply sprinkle over the ice cream.

Rose sugar is simply made by layering rose petals and sugar in a jar.

Stephen Lee, known as the HerbMeister, has enjoyed a diverse culinary career consistently interwoven with his love of herbs. He is the author of five books including **About 8 Herbs** and **Go Withs**. He owned and operated The Cookbook Cottage, an internationally-known source for rare and out-of-print cookbooks and Kentucky's only cooking school for 15 years.

Twice Chairman of the Cooking Schools and Teachers Committee of the International Association of Culinary Professionals and recipient of the 2002 International Herb Association's Business Professional of the Year Award, Stephen currently manages the Daily Lunch Program for the Homeless for the Archdiocese of Louisville. He is the Superintendent of the Culinary Department of the Kentucky State Fair, a licensed and active Auctioneer and an honest-to-goodness Kentucky Colonel. Learn more at www.herbmeister.com.

As a FINAL word for rose affectionadoes and those who love the garden here is a poem by Irishman, Thomas Moore. Written in 1805, it is now better known as the lyrics for a timeless song sung by many, such as Celtic Women, Judas Priest and most recently by Charlette Church.

The Last Rose of Summer

'Tis the last rose of summer,
Left blooming alone;
All her lovely companions
Are faded and gone;
No flower of her kindred,
No rosebud is nigh,
To reflect back her blushes,
Or give sigh for sigh.
I'll not leave thee, thou lone one!
To pine on the stem;
Since the lovely are sleeping,
Go, sleep thou with them.
Thus kindly I scatter,
Thy leaves o'er the bed,
Where thy mates of the garden
Lie scentless and dead.
So soon may I follow,
When friendships decay,
From Love's shining circle
The gems drop away.
When true hearts lie withered
And fond ones are flown,
Oh! who would inhabit,
This bleak world alone?

Jim Long showing us *How to Eat a Rose.*

Jim's Rose Recipes

Jim Long

THESE RECIPES ARE excerpted from Jim's book *How to Eat a Rose*, published by Long Creek Herbs, 2011 (new edition this year).

Raspberry and Rose Yogurt Salad Dressing

THIS IS A quick, easy salad dressing that you can mix up before you go to work, and have a healthy, low-calorie salad for lunch.

1/2 cup raspberry yogurt
1/2 teaspoon food grade rose water
2 teaspoons milk or water
1 tablespoon finely-chopped fragrant rose petals

In a small bowl, combine the yogurt, rose water, milk or water and rose petals. Blend together well and serve over mixed salad greens. This is especially good on the traditional bitter/mild European salad mixes.

It will keep for a week in the refrigerator.

THESE CAN BE as elegant and beautiful, or as simple as you choose. Make them for a special afternoon tea, even for a baby shower.

Angel food cake, ready-made, or homemade yourself
2 teaspoons rose syrup
8-ounce package cream cheese, softened
About 2 cups fragrant rose petals

Slice angel food cake into 1/2-inch thick slices with a serrated knife. (Dip the knife into warm water between slicing each piece, to make the knife slice better.)

In a small bowl, mix rose syrup with softened cream cheese.

Spread one slice of cake with softened, rose-cream cheese. Layer it with lots of rose petals, mixing colors if you have them. Add another slice of angel food cake that has also been spread with cream cheese and make a sandwich, lightly pressing the rose petals in between the slices.

Cut the sandwiches into smaller shapes, scatter a handful of rose petals over the sandwiches for garnish and serve with rose tea. This can be prepared ahead of time and refrigerated. Let come to room temperature before serving.

USE DRIED OR *fresh rose petals for this fragrant tea; it can be served hot or over ice.*

1 tea bag, black tea, like Lipton® or Luzianne®
1 heaping tablespoon fresh rose petals or 2 teaspoons dry rose petals

Place the tea and roses in a teacup. Pour 1 cup boiling water over the tea and roses. Cover with a saucer and let steep for 5 minutes. Sweeten with honey if desired.

Combining rose petals with black tea makes
for an aromatic and delicious cup.

See *Jim Long*'s bio on page 98.

Red rose petals give a brigher rosy color to sauces and infusions.

Peach Rose Sauce

Pat Crocker

SERVE THIS PRETTY sauce chilled and use as you would a jam, with fruit or cheese. Alternately, heat and drizzle it over pancakes or gingerbread. You can substitute corn syrup for the brown rice syrup.

Makes 2 1/2 cups

3 peaches, peeled and coarsely chopped
1 cup pitted fresh apricots, quartered
3 tablespoons rose water
2 tablespoons brown rice syrup
1/4 cup fresh rose petals

In a large saucepan, combine peaches, apricots, rose water and syrup. Cover and bring to a gentle boil over medium heat. Reduce heat and gently simmer for 15 minutes or until apricots are soft. Stir in rose petals. Serve warm or refrigerate until chilled.

Variation: Use orange water or apple juice in place of the rose water.

See Pat Crocker's bio on page 36.

There is a huge variety of rose water and essential oils on the market today. Use your senses--olfactory and taste buds-- to choose ones you like best.

Milk Cookies with Rose Water

Carol Little

THIS IS A special, very tasty cookie recipe from Lebanon via my brother-in-law Michel and sister Yvonne. Every family has their own traditional recipe, which is handed down through generations. "Milk cookies" are not something one buys in a store, but are always homemade. This version features "mahlab", an aromatic spice made from the crushed seed kernels of the black cherry (*Prunus mahaleb*). It has added a sweet-sour-nutty taste to biscuits, cookies and breads for centuries in several Middle Eastern cultures. In this recipe, it offers a subtle almond-cherry flavour. It also makes the dough softer, but can be omitted if you can't locate it in your local health food or Middle Eastern stores. Note: If desired, brush the tops of the cookies with beaten egg yolk for a glaze, just before baking. Use unsalted butter.

Makes 5 to 6 dozen

5 cups all-purpose flour
1/2 teaspoon black cherry kernels, finely ground (*mahlab*)
1 1/2 cups organic sugar
1/2 teaspoon salt
1/2 teaspoon allspice or cinnamon, ground
1 cup unsalted butter, clarified*, at room temperature
1/2 package yeast, dissolved in 1/4 cup warm water with a pinch of sugar
1/2 cup warm milk
2 teaspoons rose water

In a bowl, mix the flour, mahlab, sugar, salt, and allspice or cinnamon together. Add the butter a little at a time, and rub the mixture between your fingertips until crumbly.

Make an indentation in the center of this mixture. Add the dissolved yeast, milk, and rose water and start mixing gently from the center, with your fingers until all the ingredients are well mixed. (The dough should be soft like pie dough.) Cover and set aside for 1 hour.

On a floured surface, roll the dough into 3-inch rounds about 1/4-inch thick. Flute the edges with a fork and prick a design on top (or use a cookie cutter).

Place the rounds on a greased cookie sheet. Cover with a cloth and let stand for another 40 minutes. Preheat oven to 350° F about 10 minutes before baking.

Bake for approximately 15 minutes or until golden brown. Remove to baking racks to cool. Pack into tins to keep fresh, or freeze, if desired.

* To clarify butter: In a medium-sized pot, melt the butter slowly. Let it sit for a bit to separate. Skim off foam that rises to the top and gently pour the butter off from the milk solids which have settled to the bottom of the pot. Yield: 1 stick of butter (8 tablespoons) will produce about 6 tablespoons clarified butter. Many people who bake prefer using clarified butter because it gives the finished product a longer shelf life and can produce better baking results at higher temperatures.

See Carol Little's bio on page 48.

Blossom & Thorn: The Lessons of Wild Rose

Kiva Rose

I WORK WITH *Rosa* spp. extensively in my practice and have a personal affinity with it. Every May I hike through riparian canyons and mountain meadows in search of one of my most beloved plant allies. The most common local species is *Rosa woodsii*, a common Western wild rose that rambles across riverbanks, canyon walls and the borders of upper elevation swamps.

Even this year in the midst of drought and fire I found a few roses blooming. Perhaps the most striking scene was during my drive up into the White Mountains for the first time after the Wallow Fire swept through eastern Arizona and western New Mexico. There on the side of a road in the middle of the burned-out forest, surrounded by ash and blackened trees was a single Wild Rose bush, untouched and covered with late blooming flowers that were fragrant in the muggy heat of late June.

With its sweet flowers, rambling ways and formidable thorns the wild rose serves as something of a personal emblem and role model for me. In general, I tend to relate at least as well to plants as I do people and usually prefer their company, especially when I'm stressed, overtired or upset. Spending time with roses, especially the crazy haphazard hedges that grow head-high along the river here in the canyon, is both nourishing and challenging to my inherently pitta-fied ways. Their curved thorns brazenly grab and hold my skirts whenever I try to hurriedly maneuver among the plants to gather their petals... and the more I move the more tangled I end up. Until I learn to stand still and sort skirt from thorn which causes me to slow down long enough to breathe in the entirely intoxicating scent of the flowers combined with the musky aroma of the red-tinted leaves.

The medicine of rose is not only in the lessons that entangled interaction can bring, but also as a traditional remedy throughout its growing range. While often mostly thought of as a pretty flower or invasive nuisance (Multifloras), they don't always get their due in regards to clinical significance. I'd be hard pressed to imagine my practice without *Rosa's* amazing nervine, cooling, mood enhancing anti-inflammatory, anti-infective, astringent, bioflavonoid-rich medicine. Whether for gut inflammation, sunburns, anxiety or constitutional heat, this common herb's actions are widely applicable and incredibly useful. I won't belabor the point here as I've already written a great deal about this plant previously. You can check out more of my rose-centered ramblings at http://animacenter.org.

Wild Rose Birthday Feast

WHEN MY 31ST birthday rolled around recently in the second week of July we celebrated in traditional canyon feasting form, and I spent much of the day happily in the kitchen listening to Ukrainian and Romani music while cooking. For the dessert I decided to prepare Wild Rose Baklava and Spiced Wild Rose Ice Cream. Considering the drought this year, I was extra grateful that I'd stockpiled so much wild rose-infused honey over the last couple of years. The fresh flower-infused honey was the perfect consistency to blend with the crushed pecans for a flavorful yet delicate confection that was indulgent but not overly sweet.

While I certainly enjoy the traditional rosewater flavor present in many traditional baklava recipes, I have to say that the addition of wild rose to the mix definitely increased my love of this particular dish, accentuating the rich butter flavor and adding a wilder note to the whole affair. Next time around I might use the wild rose-infused honey in the nut mixture again while making a cinnamon-spiced, wild rose hip syrup to drizzle over whipped cream to top the baklava. Below you'll find my approximate recipe, as always please feel free to experiment and adapt to your personal tastes.

Rosa woodsii blooming by the
San Francisco River

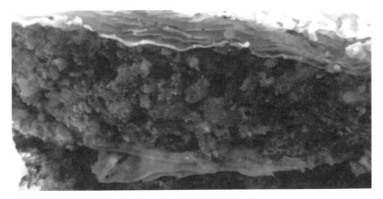

Baklava infused with wild rose honey

Wild Rose Baklava

As MOST OF my regular readers already know, I'm not one for exact recipes. Consider my instructions to be guidelines and remember to taste and adjust according to personal taste as you go along. There are many regional variations on baklava, my recipe is based loosely on Claudia Roden's Turkish recipe from her *New Book of Middle Eastern Food*.

However, mine is a creamy variation (somewhat like the Turkish *muhallebili baklava*) which helps hold the nut filling together since I use far less sugar/honey than most recipes and also includes a Persian-influenced spice blend. You can also use your favorite recipe and just substitute rose-infused honey or add rose water to the sugar syrup. Some people are intimidated by making baklava, but really, it's super simple and easy if somewhat time consuming with all that butter-brushing and dough-layering.

You can use any rose-infused honey you like the taste of—this is just standard rose petal-infused honey—you can even leave the petals in the honey if you like the texture rather than straining them out. You may want to add more honey than this; I don't care for very sweet desserts, so if you have a serious sweet tooth, you'll want to adjust. If you're using fresh rose-infused honey then the honey should be thin enough to pour and mix well. If you used dry petals, you may need to warm it in order to mix it.

Serves 6

1 /2 batch or 1/2 package phyllo dough
1 to 1 1/2 cups butter-roasted pecans (or similar nut), coarsely ground
1 to 2 tablespoons rose water, optional
1 tablespoon orange zest, finely chopped
1 teaspoon pure vanilla extract
1 teaspoon cinnamon
1/2 teaspoon freshly ground black pepper
1/2 teaspoon cardamom
1 to 2 teaspoons salt
8-ounce package cream cheese, at room temperature
1 to 2 sticks unsalted butter, melted to brush on phyllo dough (use more or less depending on how you feel about butter)
1/2 cup wild rose-infused honey

Preheat oven to 300° F. Butter an 8 inch square baking pan.

In a mixing bowl combine nuts, rose water, orange zest, vanilla, cinnamon, black pepper, cardamom, salt and 1/4 cup of the rose-infused honey. Fold in the softened cream cheese. Blend until smooth and taste for seasoning and sweetness. Add more spices, flavorings, or honey etc., to taste. Then set aside.

If using packaged phyllo dough, remove dough from package and cut approximately in half or a little larger than your pan. Whether using homemade or packaged phyllo dough, wrap one half in damp cloth so it doesn't dry out and return to a cool place.

Begin laying the sheets of phyllo dough in the pan, one at a time, brushing butter over each layer as you go. If your sheets of dough are somewhat rectangular even after cutting in half (this is normal), just layer it so that you rotate how you lay the long side in the pan so it ends up fairly even. Layer and butter half of the phyllo dough. Spread the nut and honey mixture evenly over the phyllo in the pan. Cover with the remaining phyllo dough sheets, remembering to butter between each layer.

Gathering of *Rosa woodsii* flowers and leaves

With a very sharp knife, cut diagonal parallel lines about 2 inches apart in diamond shapes; be sure to cut all the way to the bottom. At this point, I often add more butter by pouring some into the cut areas.

Of course most people bake their baklava in their oven. However, it was way too hot in our cabin to have the woodstove going so I cooked mine by putting the baking pan inside a large cast iron pan with a pot lid over it and cooked it on the propane stovetop over low heat for about 45 minutes. It worked great, and I just browned the top by warming each piece in a pan face down before serving.

Then pour remaining 1/4 cup rose honey over the top of the still warm baklava and let it soak in a bit before serving. Top with whipped cream or ice cream as you like. We ate ours warm topped with homemade wild rose ice cream while sitting in the garden with the beginning of a summer rain falling on us.

Kiva Rose is a traditional herbalist practicing and teaching in the wild mountains of southwest New Mexico. Her work as a clinician, author and artist is focused around wild plants, accessible medicine and sustaining folk herbalism locally and world-wide. She is the co-director of the Traditions in Western Herbalism Conference held each year in northern New Mexico, and co-editor and publisher of Plant Healer Magazine, an online quarterly journal of the new folk herbalism resurgence. Find out more at http://traditionsinwesternherbalism.org.

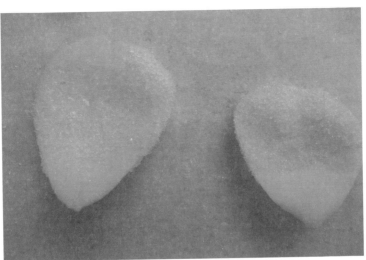

Sugaring rose petals is easy, but it takes a little time.

A Rose Eater's Guide

Skye Suter

WANT TO EAT a rose? I don't mean go out and pick one off the bush and stuff it in your mouth—but try one in an edible format for a deliciously, sweet and perfumed flavor which will please both your sense of smell and taste.

The edible parts of the rose used in cooking are the petals and the hips. The petals add a distinctive sweetness and perfume used in puddings and compotes, to make jams and sauces, and can also be candied. Rose water or rose distillate is called for in many recipes and is made from the petals. Rose hips give an added tartness to a fruit pie or jam.

Roses are widely popular, used in cuisines by many cultures through-out the world. Eastern and Middle Eastern cuisines add rose waters and rose syrups to sweets and desserts. They can be found in pastries and ice creams, crepes, fudges and fruit drinks. Medieval Europeans used rose water, rose distillations, rose petals and rose hips for household needs from scenting clothing to medicinal remedies and of course in cooking. To this day roses are used externally (for skin care) as well as internally for health (vitamin C tea) and tasty baked goods from cakes and breads to scones and tarts.

Create an added dimension to a sandwich spread or a sauce by adding a few freshly chopped rose petals. Chop up three or four scented rose petals (first removing the white base) with a brick of cream cheese for tea sandwiches. Rose petals can be added to chutney such as an apple or mango or even a duck sauce. Add rose petals to a sautéed stone fruit like a peach or nectarine for a delicious side dish or to serve over rice or noodles.

Candied or Sugared Rose Petals

ROSE PETALS CANDIED or sugared are used as an edible decoration on cakes or fruits or other desserts. When preparing petals for sugaring, remove the white portion at the base of the petal as it has a bitter flavor, which will ruin the overall taste. Sugaring rose petals is easy but takes a little time.

In a small bowl mix about 1 tablespoon of dry egg white to approximately 2 tablespoons of water. Whisk well to break up lumps of the dry egg white. The liquid should be thin and runny about the consistency of a thinned egg wash. Hold a petal with a pair of tweezers and thoroughly coat the egg white onto all areas. Place granulated sugar in a cheese shaker and sprinkle on both sides of the petal to coat. Set the petal on wax paper. Repeat with remaining petals.

Check the petals occasionally and turn them gently with the tweezers to prevent sticking and dry them evenly. They should dry completely in a day or two and can be stored in an air-tight container layered between paper towels until ready to use. They will keep a year or so if stored away in a dry and dark cupboard.

Rose Water

ROSE WATER IS beneficial topically and is used in many beauty and skin care treatments as a toner, cleanser and refreshing misting spray. Whether using roses to make a beauty aid or in a recipe make sure the petals come from a reliable source to insure purity.

Both smell and taste are integrated in the experience of eating. A great part of the pleasure of eating roses is the scent. For this reason the highly perfumed damask rose is the preferred flower for making rose water, jams or what-have-you.

To make your own rose water, take one cup of firmly packed rose petals and put them in a bowl. Pour two cups of boiling water over the petals, then cover and steep until cool. Strain and squeeze out excess liquid from the petals and store in a glass jar. Label and refrigerate and use as needed. Use this rose water within a week or two for best results.

To make the rose water into syrup, combine a two-to-one ratio of the rose water with sugar and bring it to a boil. Cook at a medium heat until it turns a nice syrupy consistency. This can be stored in the freezer indefinitely.

Rose Hips

THE OTHER PART of the rose used in cooking is the seedpod referred to as the rose hip or haw. The hip is generally harvested in the fall after a frost. This sweetens the tartness of the hip.

In our time, rose hips are often found brewing in a teacup, creating a lovely tart tea and giving us a nice dose of vitamin C. Hips also flavor foods like puddings, breads, soups, jellies, syrups, pies, and candies. Many recipes calling for rose hips also combine them with apples. Roses are actually members of the apple family. This may be why they complement each other so well.

In Great Britain during World War II importation of citrus was severely limited. The Brits avoided scurvy by collecting rose hips and concocting a sauce out of them. The government then distributed this high-in-vitamin-C syrup.

Rose hips are most commonly prepared into a puree or syrup form to use in recipes. To make a puree, combine about 4 or 5 cups of rose hips in a non-reactive pan with enough water to cover them. Bring to a boil and simmer, uncovered for about 15 to 20 minutes until the hips are well softened. Strain the hips and liquid through a sieve to remove seeds and skins and other debris. Set aside the strained puree.

If it seems that there is more to be had from the skins and hips return them to the pan with a small amount of water and repeat the process once more to get more puree. When repeating the cooking process, add a lesser amount of water than the first time.

The strained puree should be the consistency of a liquid jelly. If this is too tart, some sugar can be added to the cooking process. The puree can be used in recipes such as puddings or tarts or it can be drizzled over a pancake or waffle. The puree can also be transformed into a "leather" or chewy fruit candy.

To make the rose-hip leather, spread the puree on a cookie sheet covered with wax paper. Leave it out to cure or harden in the sun or place in a very low oven (150° to 200° F) for several hours. When it sets it can be cut and rolled up into edible portions. Store the leather in an air-tight container. It will keep for several weeks or longer.

Rose Hip and Apple Tart

THIS ROSE HIP tart is a modified rendition of a recipe from *The Accomplisht Cook or the Art and Mystery of Cookery,* a cookbook from the 17th century. The original must have caused a lot of mouth puckering because it called for a large amount of rose hips.

Makes one tart

3 cups ripe, whole rose hips (cleaned, seeds and hairs removed)
1 lemon
About 2 cups water
3 to 4 tablespoons sugar
1/2 teaspoon cinnamon
4 pieces crystallized ginger, slivered
5 baking apples, such as Empire or Granny Smith
Pastry for one tart shell
1/2 cup of your favorite jam, such as apricot or an apple jelly, thinned with a sugar syrup, water or rum, optional

Prepare the hips by cutting them in half and cleaning out seeds and hairs. Wash and pat dry.

Squeeze the juice of a lemon into a bowl and add 1 to 2 cups water; this acidulated water helps prevent the apples from discoloration.

Combine the sugar, cinnamon and ginger slivers in a bowl. Preheat the oven to 375° F.

Peel, core and slice the apples. Give the apple slices a quick dip in the acidulated water. Then toss the apples with the cinnamon sugar.

Prepare the pastry and arrange it in a tart pan. Layer the hips and apples to fill the pastry shell. Make sure the apples are the top layer so they can be attractively arranged. Sprinkle the top with about a tablespoon of sugar.

Bake in the preheated oven for 45 minutes to an hour, until the apples are tender and golden brown. Remove from oven and brush with the thinned jam or jelly. Serve warm or at room temperature.

Dried rose hips are fruity and tart in flavor.

Read *Skye Suter's* bio on page 122.

Basket of just-harvested rose petals in India

Recipes:
The Bath & Boudoir

Marge likes to use 'Minorcan' red roses from her garden.

Making Rose Soap

Marge Powell

What is Soap?

SOAP IS THE result of the combination of an acid and an alkaline base, which react together to become a neutral entity through a chemical process called saponification. The fats used in making soap are the acid portion and the alkali, which for bar soap is sodium hydroxide (NaOH), which is EXTREMELY CAUSTIC, POTENTIALLY DANGEROUS and WARRANTS EXTREME CAUTION IN HANDLING AND USE. Caustic substances burn. When mixed with water sodium hydroxide is lye.

A frequently asked question is: "Is there lye in soap?" or "Is this like my grandmother's Lye soap which was very harsh?" The answer is: soap, by definition, must be made with lye or another caustic, however, there is NO lye in the finished soap. This is because when the lye (sodium hydroxide) and the fat (fatty acids and glycerol) combine the molecular bonds are broken and recombine to form different substances. The sodium in the sodium hydroxide breaks down the fat into its components of fatty acids and glycerol. Then the fatty acids and the sodium further react to become soap. The hydroxide combines with the glycerol to become glycerin. This is the process of saponification and the result is soap and glycerin.

The reason that the old-fashioned lye soap was harsh was because it was usually made from a collection of various fats and oils collected over a period of time. Every fat has a saponification value which indicates how much lye is required to properly saponify that particular fat. Today handcrafted soap makers carefully calculate the lye required using the saponification value of each fat in the formula. When homemakers collected their fats for the old lye soap no attention was paid to the saponification value of the fats involved and the amount of lye used was a matter of guesswork and experience. If the soap was harsh it was because more lye was used than was required to saponify the collected fats.

Handcrafted soap is approximately 25 percent glycerin. There is a myth that glycerin soap is transparent soap. Chemically, this is not true. All handcrafted soap made from an acid and an alkaline base, not from purchased soap bases, is very high in glycerin. Handcrafted soap is usually not transparent (though it can be made to be transparent). Commercial transparent soaps have been tested for their glycerin content and have been found to be very low on glycerin. Commercial producers of bar soap extract the glycerin that results from their soap production because it is an economically viable by-product.

The Rose Soap

THE FOLLOWING FORMULA is for one bar of rose soap. The formula can be expanded to, for example 10 bars, by multiplying *every* ingredient by 10. A formula for a single bar of soap is convenient if you would like to experiment with other scents and ground herbs rather than those included in the rose formula. However, do not change any of the oils or the ratio of the lye to the oils. The bar of rose soap will be a cold-process soap which means that once the oils are heated no further heat is used in the process.

The major steps are:

- Mix the lye
- Combine and heat the oils
- Add the lye to the oils
- Mix to the point of trace (which is the point when you can dip a spoon in the solution and the solution has thickened enough to support the dripping from the spoon – like a thin pudding.)
- Add the rose petals and the rose scent
- Pour into the mold

Why Roses?

THERE IS A long traditional use of roses in skin care that likely dates back prior to the current era. Our soap will use roses in five different forms:

1. **Rose infused oil**: Roses have the ability to balance the pH of the skin. They are stringent but do not strip moisture from the skin. They also have antibacterial properties.

2. **Rose hip seed oil**: Is unique among vegetable oils because it contains retinol (vitamin A). Rose hip seed oil is high in the essential fatty acids - linoleic acid or omega-3, and linolenic acid or omega-6. It is helpful for a variety of skin conditions, including dermatitis, acne and eczema, for mature and sunburned skin as well as brittle nails. Use in combination with other oils.

3. **Rose water**: Is suitable for all skin types but is very helpful for dry, sensitive or aging skin. Its astringency has an effect on the capillaries just below the surface of the skin which aids in reducing the redness caused by enlarged capillaries. Rose water is also said to restore the pH balance of the skin and to prevent early aging and wrinkles.

4. **Rose petals**: Not only give the soap color and texture but have traditionally been used to soften the skin.

5. **Rose absolute**: Is the true scent of roses which is said to have both an anti-depressive and a stress reducing effect.

You will notice that your finished bar will have a golden color. This is the color of true rose based oils, such as rose hip seed oil and rose absolute which is the scent of the rose extracted from actual rose petals. We think of rose as a pink color but rose-based oils will be golden.

The Formula for Making
an Individual Bar of Rose Soap

The Oils

- 1.8 ounces rose petal infused olive oil
- 1.6 ounces coconut oil
- .2 ounces rose hip seed oil
- .4 ounces cocoa butter
- .2 ounces beeswax

The Caustic

- .6 ounces sodium hydroxide (lye) – do not use Drano or other drain cleaners!
- 1.4 ounces rose water

The Additives

- 1 tablespoon ground dried rose petals
- 10 drops rose absolute in 100 drops of jojoba oil, you can also use attar of roses or rose concrete. The jojoba oil is optional

Temperatures

- Oil - 130° F approximately
- Lye - 135° F approximately

What You will Need for The Process

- A towel
- Plastic gloves
- Eye protection
- Dried rose petals
- Wax paper
- A scale

- Rose absolute
- Small bottle – 10 ml to 1 ounce
- 1 cottage cheese container with lid
- The oils, cocoa butter and beeswax
- The lye
- Rose water
- 1 sandwich bag
- 4-ounce bottle with cap
- Small funnel that fits the neck of the bottle
- A chopstick
- Jojoba oil
- Saucepan – not aluminium
- 2 plastic spoons
- Thermometer
- Paper towels
- Bag for garbage
- A soap mold, preferably with a lid

1. Place the towel on your work space area

2. Assemble all of your equipment

3. Put on the gloves and eye protection

4. Assemble all of your ingredients

   - Grind the rose petals. Place on a piece of wax paper
   - Weigh the rose absolute into the small bottle
   - Using the cottage cheese container lid, weigh the lye on the scale
   - Gently shake the lye into the plastic bag and seal, discard the lid into the garbage bag
   - Weigh the rose water into the 4-ounce bottle
   - Weigh all of the oils into the cottage cheese container

5. Put the funnel into the neck of the 4-ounce bottle and gently sift the lye from the sandwich bag into the funnel. Use the chopstick to be sure all of the measured lye goes into the rose water.

6. Use the chopstick to dissolve all of the lye in the rose water. DO NOT HOLD THE BOTTLE BY THE BOTTOM – IT WILL BE VERY HOT!

7. Remove the chopstick and immediately cap the bottle. Set it aside where it cannot be knocked over or dropped.

8. Pour all of your oils, cocoa butter and beeswax into the saucepan. Reserve the cottage cheese container.

9. Heat the oils on medium heat until just before all of the beeswax is melted. Remove the pan from the heat and stir to complete the melting of the beeswax.

10. Pour your melted oils back into the cottage cheese container. Note the temperature. Wipe the pan out thoroughly with paper towel.

11. Take the temperature of the lye/rose water mix. If both temperatures are in the range of 130° F (if they are above 150° F wait for them to cool down, if they are below 130° F pour anyway), slowly pour the lye/rose water mix into the oils in the cottage cheese container. BE CAREFUL OF SPLASHING.

12. Stir with the plastic spoon until the soap begins to trace, then stir in your additives and essential oil.

13. Scrape all of the soap mixture into your mold. Discard the cottage cheese container into the garbage.

14. Cover the mold with the lid.

What You Will Do Next

Let the soap in the mold sit undisturbed for 24 hours, covered.

Uncover the mold and place in the freezer for 3 to 8 hours.

Remove the mold from the freezer and unmold it onto a piece of towel or washcloth.

Let the unmolded bar sit for about 3 days on the cloth.

Put the bar into a basket or something else where air can circulate and tuck it away for about 4 weeks.

After 4 weeks, trim off any rough edges and polish with a soft cloth.

Then – Enjoy!

Rose Soap, the finished product

The rose mold is from Milky Way Molds http://www.milkywaymolds.com

Oils:

http://soaperschoice.com/

http://www.mountainroseherbs.com

Soapmaking supplies – no minimum order

http://www.snowdriftfarm.com/

http://www.brambleberry.com/

Scents – minimum order required

http://www.libertynatural.com/

http://www.essentialoil.com/

Marge Powell has been an herbalist for over 25 years and an avid plant person her entire life. Her herbal interests span the culinary, the medicinal and body care. She has conducted hands-on workshops on a variety of herbal topics across the U.S. She is currently a board member of the IHA, the IHA Foundation and is past president of IHA's former Southeastern Region. She has had numerous herbal articles published in IHA's annual Herb of the Year publications. Marge can be contacted at: http://www.magnoliahillsoap.com

Rose and Lavender Bath Herbs

Donna Frawley

I DEVELOPED THIS recipe to go with two other herbal baths that I sell separately, or in a Pamper Gift Box along with a candle and some chocolates.

Makes about 5 cups

1 ounce rose petals
1 ounce lavender flowers
1 ounce rolled oats
1/2 ounce orange peel
1/2 ounce lemon peel
1 tablespoon rosemary
2 bay leaves, crumbled

Measure all ingredients into a large bowl and blend well to mix. Put 3 tablespoons of the blend in a cloth bag. Put the bag in a large bowl and pour 2 cups boiling water over the bag. Let it steep for 5 minutes.

While the bag of bath herbs is steeping, transfer the remaining blend into a jar or zip-close bag and seal, then label. Pour the "tea" into the bathtub while filling with water of desired temperature. Lay back and relax.

Read *Donna Frawley's* bio on page 154.

Rose buds make a pretty and fragrant potpourri.

Rose Potpourris

Davy Dabney

Moist Potpourri

THIS IS AN old recipe for moist potpourri. Victorian housewives kept a container in the bath. They removed the lid when fragrance was desired. This should last for several years. If more fragrance is desired, a few drops of essential oil may be added.

3 cups orange or other fragrant flowers
3 cups rose petals
3 cups carnation petals
About 6 tablespoons un-iodized salt

Mix petals together in a large bowl. Scatter 3 cups of the mixed petals into a three-gallon crock. Sprinkle 2 tablespoons of salt evenly over the petals. Place 3 more cups in the crock and sprinkle 2 more tablespoons of salt over them. Scatter the remaining petals in the crock and top off with 2 more tablespoons of salt.

Place a large glass or ceramic plate on top of the petals and place a brick, or a heavy can, on top of the plate so that the plate is weighted and pressing down on the petals.

After two weeks, remove the brick and the plate. Stir the petals to mix thoroughly. Replace the plate and brick.

After two more weeks, remove brick and plate. There will be some liquid in the bottom of the crock. Mix everything well. The mix may not be broken down enough, so replace the plate and brick and leave for another week. Check again. Stir. The petals should be clumped together. Add the following ingredients; they may be either fresh or dried.

1 cup each: marjoram, lemon thyme, myrtle leaves
1/2 cup each: mint leaves and lavender flowers
6 bay leaves, crumbled
2 tablespoons grated lemon rind
2 tablespoons ground cloves

Blend the marjoram, lemon thyme, myrtle, mint, lavender, bay leaves, lemon rind and cloves with the petals. Stir vigorously until everything is incorporated well. Cover again with the plate and brick. Stir every 3 days for about two weeks. Add up to 25 drops of orange essential oil or rose fragrance. Stir again and put into attractive ceramic containers with lids.

Dry Potpourri

USE GOOD QUALITY fragrance oils. Rose, musk, citrus or your favorite perfume may also be used. Make sure all plant material is dry before mixing!

2 tablespoons crushed (not powdered) orris root
20 drops of essential oil

Blend the orris root with up to 20 drops of essential oil—use one kind or a blend of up to 3 different oils. Put into covered glass container and set aside for 2 weeks or longer.

1 quart colorful rose petals
2 cups lavender flowers
4 ounces coriander leaves
1/2 cup crushed cinnamon sticks
1/4 cup crushed nutmeg

When the mix has had time to mellow, in a large container carefully mix the rose petals, lavender flowers, coriander leaves, cinnamon sticks, and crushed nutmeg together with the orris root and essential oils. Put into ornamental containers or clear easy-close plastic bags.

Remove petals from the roses to facilitate drying.

Davy Dabney is a founding member of the IHA (originally called Herb Growers and Marketing Association), Kentucky Herb Association, Kyana Unit of the Herb Society of America and owner of Dabney Herbs. She conducts workshops and classes and digs in the dirt, plants and harvests herbs and occasionally weeds.

Carol uses both the petals and the leaves in her potpourri

Aromatic Rose and Herb Potpourri

Carol Little

AN AROMATIC POTPOURRI can be created with the following formula. This old-fashioned recipe has many variations but this basic mixture can change the ambiance in a room and invite tranquility. Start with this simple blend below and experiment by adding tiny amounts of cloves, cinnamon powders or boost the floral with a drop or two of essential oils.

1 part rose petals
1 part lavender flowers
1 part lemon verbena leaves
1/2 part rose leaves

Combine all of the ingredients, mixing well, in a large bowl. Add the oils, if using, one drop at a time. Place into a jar with a tight-fitting lid and allow to cure for 4 to 6 weeks. Shake the jar daily.

Beautiful displayed in a shallow bowl, this potpourri transforms any room; bed, bath, boudoir, office or living space with its gentle aroma. Store any extra in a covered container in a cool place.

Whatever way roses find their way into your life, they will be sure to add a sweet fragrance, a glorious poetic complement to your garden, an exhilaration when they over-winter (for some of us!) and perhaps above all, a certain tranquil peace when they find their way into your life as an uplifting and soothing medicine.

Read Carol Little's bio on page 48.

Home distillation of rose water

Recipes: The Apothecary

Freshly-made rose and
apple cider vinegar,
'Lady Banksia' roses

The rose and herb vinegar has
turned a deep ruby red.

Roses in Your Vinegar

Marge Powell

FOR MANY PEOPLE venturing into the world of herbs, their first experiments are infused herbal vinegars. But after a few batches they give them up because many people do not know how and where to use the infused vinegars or the nutritional benefits they hold.

There is a very special herb-infused vinegar that is made with rose petals and I like to add the flowering parts of rosemary and thyme to the mix. The rose petals must be organically grown and free of any sprays. The mechanics of creating the infused vinegar are basic, but understanding why you would want to keep this vinegar as one of your culinary assets requires explanation.

First consider the medicinal value of the vinegar. The acid in the vinegar, over time, helps release the vitamins and minerals from the plant cells. The rose petals contain vitamin C. There are old remedies that use an infusion of rose petals to relieve cold and flu symptoms. There has been a Danish study that suggests rose petals, as well as rose hips, have anti-inflammatory properties. So after a few weeks, what has started out as cider vinegar with plants in it becomes cider vinegar with vitamin C. And should you add a sprig or two of flowering thyme and rosemary, you have added more vitamin C as well as vitamin A and calcium and potassium.

But then how do we use this vitamin-enriched vinegar? My suggestion is to taste your vinegar after it has infused for 4 to 6 weeks and tap into your intuitive sense of the taste. We do this when we say to ourselves "Oh, this would taste good with _____". A good way to taste infused vinegar is to pour a very small amount of the vinegar in to a saucer then place a sugar cube in the saucer just long enough for the sugar cube to absorb some vinegar. Then suck the vinegar from the sugar cube and discard the sugar cube. When I taste rose petal-infused vinegar I get a light, slightly flowery taste and I sense that this would go well with fruit. Vinegar and fruit is not a common combination, but vinegar seems to make the taste of fruit come alive.

Try sprinkling some of this vinegar over fresh cut strawberries, or watermelon, or over pears before they are poached; you will definitely notice the difference. Another way to use the vinegar is deglazing a pan of sautéed chicken. Remove the cooked chicken from the sauté pan and add 2 tablespoons of the vinegar to the pan juices, stir to loosen the browned bits, and then pour over the chicken. I would also add a couple of tablespoons of this vinegar to soup, especially a light chicken-based soup or even a tomato bisque.

Then there is the visual treat of the vinegar. If you use a red shade of rose petals for your vinegar, the vinegar will gradually turn a very rosy color. If you decant the vinegar after 4 to 6 weeks, you will have a bottle of vinegar the color of rosé wine.

Rose Petal-Infused Vinegar

Makes about 1 quart

You will need:

- ⁃ Clean glass container such as quart Mason jar or a bottle
- ⁃ Non-metallic lid or cork
- ⁃ Enough fresh, organic rose petals to fill your container
- ⁃ 1 sprig of flowering thyme (optional)
- ⁃ 1 sprig of flowering rosemary (optional)
- ⁃ Cider vinegar, preferably organic (do not use white distilled vinegar)

The process:

Pack the rose petals and the rosemary and thyme (if you are using them) into the glass container. Pack as many as will fit. A wooden chopstick is a handy tool if you are packing the petals into a narrow-neck bottle. Cover the plant material with the vinegar, place the lid on the container and turn upside down for a few seconds. This is an important step because air has been trapped among the petals and turning the bottle upside down helps the trapped air to escape. Then top off the container with more vinegar. It is important that all plant material is always covered with vinegar or mold will develop. As the container sits for the first few days more air will rise to the top.

Store the container where you can see it for the first week and check it periodically to be sure the vinegar covers the plant material, if it does not—top off the container with more vinegar. Let the vinegar sit for 4 to 6 weeks. After this time it is ready to use.

The vinegar can be decanted by straining it into another container and discarding the plant material. Label the vinegar. Or do not decant it and use it with the plant material in the container. I find that it makes only an aesthetic difference. The vinegar will keep at least one year.

You may want to experiment beyond the culinary with your rose vinegar using the recipe suggestions below.

Rose Vinegar Facial Toner

ROSES HAVE BEEN traditionally used to soften the skin and apple cider vinegar has traditionally been used to refresh and tone the skin. Rose vinegar brings these two elements together.

Note: before using any product on your skin, test it first by applying to the skin on the inside of your elbow. Wait 24 hours. If any redness occurs do not use the product on your skin.

- 1 cup distilled water
- 2 tablespoons rose vinegar

Mix the vinegar and water. Apply to your face with a blotting action and a cotton pad. Wait 10 minutes and rinse with cool water. Discard any remaining toner.

VINEGAR HAS OFTEN been used as a hair conditioner to restore the pH of hair after the alkaline effects of hair coloring and shampoos and to leave hair "squeaky clean". You can use the rose vinegar as a restorative hair rinse.

Using an old, but clean shampoo bottle or another plastic "squeeze" type bottle add 2 tablespoons of rose vinegar. After shampooing, add warm water to the vinegar in the bottle (cold water may be a bit of a shock) and rinse your hair with the vinegar/water mix. You can either rinse again with clear water or leave the vinegar rinse in your hair.

As everyone's hair is different, you will need to experiment with the ratio of vinegar and water and whether to leave the rinse in your hair after shampooing.

Healing Spirits' homegrown and dried, red rose petals

Read *Marge Powell's* bio on page 196.

Rose Recipes from Healing Spirits' Apothecary

Andrea and Matthias Reisen

Rose Petals in Glycerine

A FEW YEARS ago a friend, Carol Simons, was visiting and she gave me a taste of rose petals in vegetable glycerine. I was in LOVE. I went right outside my door to the *Rosa rugosa* plant and made some of my own. I have tried making this with other roses and it's okay, but nothing tastes as good to me as the *Rosa rugosa*.

I think of roses for the heart, and this was confirmed by my son-in-law. My son-in-law is a big outdoors-kind-of-guy, tattoos, chainsaws, etc. He walked in the house, I said open your mouth, he did, I put a dropper of the Rose Petal in Glycerine in his mouth, he leaned back against the wall and said "What was that? It's too strong—it went right to my heart—I can feel it in my heart!" I have given him a bottle of his own so he can take it at his own pace, when he feels the need to open his heart.

Makes about 1 pint

About 1 1/2 cups vegetable glycerin
1 to 2 cups fresh rose petals

In a pint jar, fill it less than 3/4 full with vegetable glycerine. Then, every day, pick what rose petals are opened and continue filling the jar until not another one will fit into it. This may take a few days depending on how many rose bushes you have. Allow the infusion to stand for about two weeks, shaking it every day at least once, and putting your energy into the mixture. Strain, rebottle and label. We take a bit whenever the heart is feeling a little stressed. My theory in life is you can take too little—but not too much.

Rose Flower Essence

THERE ARE MANY ways to make flower essences, this is my way that was taught to me by a dear friend. If you don't have a source of pure well water, then use bottled spring water, or distilled; don't use chlorinated water.

Gather the things needed to prepare a flower essence:

- Sunny day
- 1 to 3 roses
- Clean snippers
- Glass bowl *(I use one that was gifted to me by my Grandmother. In the early '60s she lived in Palm Springs, California. She placed this glass bowl on her roof for six months; the sun was so intense it turned the bowl amethyst in color. I like using objects that have special meaning to me, I can't touch the bowl without thinking of my Grandmother with love and the power of the sun to transform.)*
- Good water *(We have wonderful well water on our farm, I love using our water. There's also a nice spring a few miles from our house that has lovely water, which I feel inclined to use once in a while. Use water that feels alive to you, that doesn't have chlorine, etc., in it.)*
- Clean pint jar and lid
- 1-ounce dropper bottle, or whatever your personal preference is
- Brandy or apple cider vinegar *(I like using an organic cider made with the mother.)*

On a sunny day at about 10 a.m. in the morning I will go out to my rose bush, sit with it a bit, think about the roses, the essences I am going to make, and thank the roses for their beauty and what they have to offer the world before I snip them.

I have my bowl about half-filled with water, and depending on my feelings will put 1 to 3 roses in the bowl of water. I will then leave the bowl with the roses till about 2 p.m. in the afternoon. We have dogs, cats, birds, children running around, insects flying and nothing has ever landed in the bowl with the water and flowers. I will then take the roses out of the water, thank the roses for their gift, and put the water in a pint jar, filling it half way.   Then to preserve the essences, I fill the rest of the jar with brandy or apple cider vinegar.

This jar is called the mother of the flower essences. I then take a 1-ounce bottle, fill it about one-fourth full with brandy or apple cider vinegar, filling the rest of the bottle with good water, then add about 10 drops from the Mother Flower Essences. Put the dropper on the bottle and you are ready to use or gift your Rose Flower Essence. As you can see the Mother bottle will make enough Rose Flower Essence for a *long* time, so enjoy the bounty in abundance. Share with friends and family, have them share with you how it makes them feel, tell your own stories.

The rose is a symbol of love. The flower essences help you to open to love, and bring your desires into action.

Healing Spirts' make their own rose glycerite and flower essence.

LIQUEURS ARE SUCH fun to make and to experiment with. At the 2011 International Herb Symposium in Midland, Michigan we gave a talk on chocolate which involved sampling many different chocolates and a chocolate liqueur sweetened with rose glycerite, and a liqueur of rose, damiana *(Turnera aphrodisiaca)* and chocolate sweetened with maple syrup. The base for these liqueurs was 80 proof or 40 percent alcohol. I used an inexpensive vodka, but you can use whatever you like. Here is a simple recipe for you to start with but please don't be afraid to experiment.

Makes about 1 quart

About 1 cup rose petals
About 1 cup damiana leaves
About 1 cup dark chocolate, finely grated or cocoa powder
About 3 cups vodka
Honey, maple syrup or rose glycerite

Start with a quart jar and fill two -thirds full with equal parts rose petals, damiana and chocolate. I used raw chocolate from Jamaica but any organic cocoa or fine quality chocolate will work. Pour the vodka over the mixture in the jar, cover with a non-reactive lid, and place in a sunny window for at least two weeks, shaking daily and putting your energy into the mixture. I occasionally open the lid to make sure that there is no formation of gases in the jar.

After two weeks, (you can definitely let it set longer if you wish), drain the herbs out of the liquid. You might have some sediment from the chocolate which you can filter out with a fine filter or siphon the liquid off as if you were bottling wine. I tend to leave my sediment in my liqueur feeling that it adds extra essence from the plants.

Now, add a sweetener such as honey, maple syrup or rose glycerite to taste. Pour in a pretty bottle and label; this makes a delightful after-dinner drink or a wonderful gift for a friend.

The flavor and fragrance of rose makes a lovely liqueur or cordial.

Andrea and Matthias Reisen have been community herbalists for over 20 years. They co-founded Healing Spirits Herb Farm and Education Center located in the Finger Lakes region of western New York. They have been producing high-quality, certified organic, medicinal herbs, both fresh and dried, for shipment throughout the United States and abroad. They have created their own line of valued products under the Healing Spirits label and also produce Rosemary Gladstar's line of quality products. Former Peace Corp volunteers in the Philippines, Matthias has consulted overseas in Belarus, Nepal and Jamaica regarding medicinal and aromatic plants. Andrea has studied numerous body therapies and is certified as a Zero Balancing Therapist. Together they have raised five children; there are three generations living on the farm. Their common goal is to live and work in balance and harmony with Mother Nature and humankind. www.healingspiritsherbfarm.com herbs@healingspiritsherbfarm.com

Rose petal honey is easily prepared and nutritious.

Rose Medicine

Carol Little

ROSE PETALS AND to a greater extent, rose hips (the delicious fruit) are known to be high in vitamin C, and also contain vitamins A, B-3, D and E as well as bioflavonoids, minerals, malic and citric acid. Rose hips contain pectin.

These combinations of constituents are the reason why many herbalists use rose medicine to clear toxins and heat from the body and relieve fluid retention or congestion. Rose creates "movement" in the body so it can be used to relieve heavy menstrual periods caused by uterine congestion and as a part of a diuretic or laxative formula.

Rose medicine is also known to support the liver and gall bladder, as well as the promotion of bile flow, which in turn, contributes to better elimination. Rich in vitamins, it stimulates the immune system, helps fight infections, soothes mucous membranes and can help to relieve colds and flu.

Roses have been cherished for centuries for their uplifting, healing qualities. They are believed to soothe the emotions and balance the mind. Elixir of Rose has been used effectively through the ages to comfort sorrow and relieve heartache.

I believe that rose medicine has an uplifting effect on the entire nervous system and I often include *Rose Tincture* in formulae to address concerns about sadness, grief, depression, anxiety or insomnia.

In times of deep sadness, in my own life or for my friends or clients, I have used Rose medicine accompanied by appropriate Bach Flower Remedy® flower essences with good success. I often combine the Bach Flower remedies with herbal medicine or healing foods. Whether it be in the form of tincture, tea, syrup, infused honey, vinegar, glycerite or elixir; I find adding a flower essence to the herbal remedy adds another emotional healing component needed during difficult times.

I use rose tincture and both hot and cold infusions made from rose petals and rose hips in my herbal practice.

Rose Petal Tincture

THERE ARE A great many ideas and formulas for creating the perfect tincture. Normally, in clinical practice, I use such a formula based on weights and measurements. There are a few exceptions, for me, personally. Rose Tincture –too magical in many ways – is different. I use fresh rose petals at the height of their blooming season (June for my Toronto gardens). One would only use roses from plants that have not been sprayed with chemicals. I use the petals, plucking them gently from the plant, leaving the rose hips intact to mature and bring joy in the fall. Tinctures can be created using any number of 'extraction liquids' or menstruums; vodka, brandy, grain alcohol for example. Brandy makes a lovely choice in this case. I used vodka, this year, but use what is available to you.

Makes about 1 pint

Scant pint of rose petals, lightly packed
About 1 pint of alcohol: brandy or vodka

Gather fresh rose petals. Chop the petals (or not) and place into a clean canning jar. Fill the jar with the petals; don't over-stuff.

Fill the jar to the very top with alcohol. It's important to completely cover the plant material. Cap with a tight-fitting lid, preferably a plastic one. Label the jar with the name of herb, date, plus menstruum used. Put the jar into a cool cupboard. Shake at least once a day Ready to use with delight in 4 to 6 weeks.

ALSO KNOWN AS tea or tisane. It's easy to include rose hips in infusions, either on their own or in combination with other herbs in a formula. I use rose hips with or without their seeds. Infused rose hips produce a tart, slightly acidic-tasting tea.

Diluted, I have used this for a gentle eyewash. Compresses made using rose a hip infusion can soothe a throbbing headache, and ease the pain of a sore ankle, knee or wrist. *Use the best quality water available to you.*

Makes 1 cup

1 cup water
1 tablespoon rose hips, dried (2 tablespoons if using fresh)
Pour boiling water over the rose hips in a cup or mug.

I prefer to use canning jars with lids for any infusions. The lids allow the healing constituents in the steam to remain with the tea. It's best to allow it to steep, covered for 12 to15 minutes.

Strain. Enjoy with or without sweetening.

If using as a compress, store the tea in the fridge for up to 2 days, if necessary. I prefer to make fresh batches daily, if possible.

WHETHER OUT IN the garden or enjoying a summer's day on my porch, one of my preferred thirst quenchers is a fragrant, ruby-red infusion of rose hips, hibiscus flowers and delightful lemon-scented "Melissa", lemon balm. I rarely add honey, however just a little honey does make this refreshing for everyone!

1 part rose hips
1 part hibiscus flowers
1 part lemon balm leaves
1/2 part orange peel, optional

When I make tea at home, if wanting more than a one-cup serving, I use two, 1-liter canning jars with lids. That's me… you can use a teapot or a tea press or whatever works.

To make 1 liter/quart of this tea, place 3 to 4 tablespoons of the mixture into a 1-liter/quart canning jar. Add freshly boiled water to fill the jar. Immediately cover with the lid (plastic screw-top lids make this easy). Allow to steep 12 to15 minutes.

Strain the infusion into the second canning jar. Top with lid. Allow to come to room temperature, refrigerate and/or add ice cubes. Serve with fresh lemon balm leaves as a garnish if available. Enjoy within two days!

Kiddie Calm Summertime Tea

WHEN I HAD the pleasure of nourishing Toronto's West End with herbal treasures in my shop, Studio Botanica, one of my best-selling tea blends was a gentle calming blend made especially for children. It is delicious served hot or cold. Parents loved this yummy nutritious tea as an alternative to sugary fruit juices. Some even made a version of an "herbsicle" and it was a hit with the entire neighbourhood.

1 part rose hips
1 part hibiscus flowers
1 part chamomile flowers
1 part lemon balm leaves
1/2 part catnip leaves
1/2 part milky oat tops
1/2 part spearmint leaves
1/2 part orange peel

In a bowl, combine ingredients to blend well, transfer to a jar, and label. Store in a cool, dark cupboard.

To make 1 liter/quart of this tea, place 3 to 4 tablespoons of the mixture into a 1-liter/quart canning jar. Add freshly boiled water to fill the jar. Immediately cover with the lid (plastic screw-top lids make this easy). Allow to steep 12 to15 minutes.

Strain the infusion into the second canning jar. Top with lid. Enjoy warm or refrigerate to create a tasty cold tea for adults and children alike!

LAST YEAR, FOR the first time, I infused some red wine with dried rose hips as an experiment. I had heard that this concoction can increase blood flow and digestion as a kind of 'aperitif. Since then, I've played with this basic idea with the addition of various carminative herbs. I have used cinnamon, cloves, and cardamom so far with tasty results.

Makes 1 liter/quart

4 ounces dried rose hips
1 liter/quart of full-bodied red wine
Spices, optional

Steep the dried rose hips in the red wine for 2 to 3 weeks.

Add the complementing herbs/spices after the first week. When ready to drink, strain the botanicals from the wine.

Drink a glass before your evening meal. I love to play with flavours. What would you try?

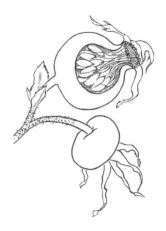

See *Carol Little*'s Bio on page 48.

Medicinal

Dorene Petersen lying (literally!) on a bed of roses.

Essential Oil of Rose

Dorene Petersen

*"And the woodbine spices are wafted abroad,
And the musk of the rose is blown."*

—*"Maud,"* Tennyson (1809-1892)

Latin Name

Rosa damascena

Family

Rosaceae

Common Names

Bulgarian rose and damask rose

Sources

THERE ARE MORE than 250 rose species, but the three primarily distilled for rose essential oil are *Rosa damascena*, *Rosa centifolia*, and *Rosa gallica*. *R. damascena* is cultivated and produced mainly in Bulgaria, as well as regions of Turkey and, to a lesser extent, in Tunisia, China, and India. In France, *R. gallica* is the species usually grown for perfume. *R. centifolia* is also distilled in small quantities in Morocco.

See an image of *R. centifolia* at the British Institute of Perfumers Web site at: http://www.bsp.org.uk/gallery_full.php?id=7

History

THE WORD ROSA comes from the Greek word *rodon*, meaning red, and the rose used by the Greeks was a deep crimson color. Referred to as the "Queen of Flowers" by the Greek poet Sappho, the Greeks cultivated the rose and the Romans made extensive use of it. The petals were used to cover floors, baths were filled with rose petals, and roses were scattered at feasts and beneath chariot wheels. Avicenna first prepared rose water in the 10th century and the oil of rose was discovered between 1582 and 1612.

An enchanting story is told of the discovery of rose oil: At the wedding feast of Shah Jahan, who built the Taj Mahal and Shalimar Gardens for his wife, a canal circling the whole garden was dug and filled with water and rose petals. The heat of the sun separated the water from the essential oil of rose. The bridal pair observed this when they were rowing on the fragrant water; the oil was skimmed off and found to be an exquisite perfume, thus beginning rose distillation in India.

There is an old custom of hanging a rose over a dinner table to ensure dinner conversation will be held in confidence. This comes from the folktale that Cupid gave a rose to the God of Silence as a bribe, so that the God of Silence would not reveal the amorous ways of Venus.

Initially, rose oil was the by-product of rose water, which was the primary product.

Parts Used

THE FRESH FLOWERS of the damask rose, *R. damascena*, and other species are used to produce rose oil. It takes 30 handpicked flowers, or about 2,000 petals, to yield 1 drop of rose essential oil. *R. damascena* yields the essential oil known as *otto* of rose, or *attar* of rose. Attar means "essential oil" in Arabic. *R. damascena* is steam distilled from the whole flower petals minus the calyx. "May" rose is an absolute grade that is produced from a concrete extraction of *R. centifolia*.

Women harvesting roses in Turkey.

Cultivation

ROSES FLOURISH BEST in a sandy or light, stony soil in full sun, and with good drainage. They are grown from either roots or cuttings planted out in rows in autumn or the early spring. In the first year, no flowers appear and only a few appear in the second year. More flowers appear in the third year, with a maximum between the fourth and tenth years. The rose is rejuvenated after 10 seasons by removing the branches and as new shoots appear, the crop is rejuvenated and harvested in the second year.

Rose trees can be productive from anywhere between 10 to 30 years. A half-acre of land will hold about 5,000 roses and can produce 2,200 pounds of flowers during a season. Experts hold that roses cultivated at altitudes of 1,000 to 2,700 feet in the Balkans are superior to any grown in plains areas.

Harvesting and Production

HARVESTING TAKES PLACE in the late spring or early summer. The weather during the rose harvest greatly influences the quality and quantity of the oil. Dry, hot weather usually gives a poorer yield.

In Turkey roses are grown on hillsides in long, horizontal, evenly spaced rows. Women with large wicker baskets hanging down their fronts and secured by back straps quickly move along the rows plucking the flowers. Plucking just the flower with no leaves or stem and avoiding the thorns is a skilled technique. The presence of leaves or stem reduces the value that the distiller will pay for the crop. The flowers are delivered to the distillery and are distilled on the same day. Women start to gather the rose flowers in the very early morning before the sun rises, and they complete the harvest before the midday sun has started to evaporate the volatile constituents, reducing the aromatic quality.

The yield is quite low. To obtain 1 pound of oil, about 10,000 pounds of rose flowers have to be distilled. Rose oil is either steam or water distilled.

Distilled rose oil is called rose otto or rose attar.

Rose absolutes are also produced but not as common. The volatile components are extracted by solvents or carbon dioxide extraction of the rose petals. The yield of oil from a solvent extraction is approximately 24 percent of the weight of the flowers and is more efficient than steam distillation. However, the extraction method can impact the active constituents found in the final product.

For aromatherapy purposes the steam-distilled rose is preferred. An absolute that is extracted using a "green" solvent, such as ethanol or carbon dioxide, can also be used for external application if a distilled rose is unavailable. Not to be ingested.

Rose market in India.

Characteristics

DISTILLED ROSE OIL is a pale yellow with an occasional green tinge. The absolute is a viscous liquid ranging from olive-yellow to brownish, orange-red. Distilled rose essential oil has a sweet, yet spicy floral aroma. At ordinary temperatures, it should form a semi-solid crystalline mass. The taste is slightly bitter at high concentrations, but becomes very pleasant in extreme dilution. It leaves no stain on the perfume blotter and feels slightly oily when rubbed between the fingers.

It should be stored in a cool place in airtight containers and protected from light. It separates into white or colorless blades of crystals at temperatures below 21°C (70°F).

Identifiable quality standards for rose oil include:

Congealing Point: +18° to 23.5
Specific Gravity: +At 20°/15° .856 to .870
Optical Rotation: -1° to -4°
Refractive Index: At 25° 1.452 to 1.466
Solubility in Alcohol: Even in 90% alcohol slightly soluble giving turbid mixtures

Adulteration

BECAUSE ROSE OIL is so expensive, it is frequently adulterated. Synthetic oil is often passed as natural rose oil. Adulterants that may be used are geraniol and l-citronellol extracted from geranium oil. This adulteration is difficult to detect through chemical analysis. Careful olfactory tests may detect their presence. Gildemeister[1] says that guaiac, *Bulnesia sarmienti*, wood oil is also used as an adulterant but this can be detected with a microscope when the oil is cooled and crystallized. The guaiac

---

1.   Gildemeister, E., Hoffmann, F., Kremers, E. (1900). *The Volatile Oils*, Volume 11. Milwaukee: Pharmaceutical Review Publishing Co: 574.

wood oil crystals are long with a canal-like groove in the middle while a rose crystal is smaller and thinner with sharply articulated shapes.

A remarkable difference between synthetic and natural rose oil is that synthetic rose is almost entirely deodorized by iodine, while natural rose oil is unaffected.

To assess the strength of rose oil, try the following test:

Drop an equal amount of oil from a number of different sources onto perfume blotters. Mark each perfume blotter with the source. Leave them at room temperature in identical environmental conditions. For 10 consecutive days, check the aroma between 10 a.m. and 11 a.m.

Record the results with the following point allocation: strong = three points, medium = two points, and weak = one point. After the tenth day, add the points. Those oils with the highest points are most likely unadulterated.

Another olfactory test that helps to confirm the results of the strength test is the bouquet test. Take your samples of rose oil that you have sourced from different suppliers and, in clean brandy glasses, add 1 drop of rose oil to 3.5 ounces of distilled water at 108° F. Use the same oils that you used for the strength test. Examine each glass carefully by inhaling deeply and slowly, and place them in order of preference. Repeat the process every hour for six hours, then again the following morning. Note the order after each examination. You will most likely find that certain samples consistently take first place. Now cross-reference your results with the strength test.

Active Constituents

STEAM-DISTILLED ROSE OIL contains more than 275 constituents, including:

The terpene alcohols geraniol, l-citronellol, nerol (5%), and l-linalool. Geraniol and citronellol suggest an antiseptic, antibacterial, antiviral, and germicidal effect.

The phenols eugenol (1%) and methyl eugenol: eugenol and the sesquiterpenes may be responsible for the topical analgesic effect.

The aldehydes citral and nonyl aldehyde.Rhodinol, which is also called l-citronellol, is present in high-quality oil from 40-65%. The alcohols also occur in ester form, such as geranyl acetate.

Up to 3% phenylethyl alcohol is sometimes found in traces, but is usually lost in the distillation water because of its water solubility. Rose absolute, which is extracted with a solvent, contains more phenylethyl alcohol; Gildemeister in *The Volatile Oils*, Volume 11, says this is an important aromatic ingredient and without it rose does not truly correspond to the natural perfume of the true rose. This is why rose hydrosol is such a wonderful aromatic product with many therapeutic, culinary, and perfumery applications.

Phenylethyl alcohol (78.38%) was found to be the main constituent of rose absolute, while citronellol and geraniol were the major compounds (>55%) of rose essential oil. The rose absolute contains more beta-carotene and vitamin E (alpha and gamma tocopherol) than the essential oil[2].

Traces of sesquiterpenes have also been found with azulene-like qualities.

It also contains about 2% of a sesquiterpene alcohol and farnesol, which has an analgesic effect and is an important constituent for perfumery.

Also important for perfumery are the esters, the nerol, the nonyl aldehyde, and trace constituents, such as carvone and rosefuran.

---

2   Ulusoy S, Boşgelmez-Tinaz G, Seçilmiş-Canbay H. (2009). Tocopherol, carotene, phenolic contents and antibacterial properties of rose essential oil, hydrosol and absolute. *Curr Microbiol*, 59(5):554-8. Epub 2009 Aug 18.

Therapeutic Actions

ANALGESIC (TOPICAL), ANTHELMINTIC, antibacterial, antidepressant, antifungal, anti-inflammatory, antimicrobial, antiphlogistic, antiseptic, antiviral, aphrodisiac, astringent, bactericidal, cholagogue, cosmetic, deodorant, depurative, disinfectant, diuretic, emmenagogue, febrifuge, germicidal, hypotensive, hepatic, narcotic, nervine, stomachic, tonic, and vulnerary.

Medicinal Uses

THE TOPICAL ANALGESIC action of rose essential oil coupled with its antibacterial and antifungal actions provides a powerful but pleasant-smelling therapeutic application with potential supportive application for: Abrasions, abscesses, acne, boils, bronchitis, burns, candida, capillaries (fragile), conjunctivitis, dermatitis, eczema, eye inflammation, rashes, sores, tinea, thrush (oral), and mouth and tongue ulcers.

For use with any infections, ensure the rose is diluted at a 2 percent dilution in boiled, cooled water and applied as a compress using sterile gauze. Additional skin support for broken capillaries and potential UV protection[3] has been suggested, primarily due to the presence of flavonoids. The infusion of rose petals may yield more flavonoids than the distilled oil.

Other potential support that would require inhalation or a few drops on a sugar cube, lactose tablet, or in a small quantity of milk include a range of respiratory issues such as coughs, fever, hay fever, throat (sore), and tonsillitis. The latter would be best supported with gargling the diluted oil in boiled, cooled water.

Digestive and urinary system issues can also be supported by rose oil such as diarrhea, flatulence, fluid retention, gallbladder (congestion),

---

3   Tabrizi H, Mortazavi SA, Kamalinejad M. (2003). An in vitro evaluation of various Rosa damascena flower extracts as a natural antisolar agent. Int J Cosmet Sci., 25(6):259-65.

headache, indigestion, nausea, and urinary tract infection. Can be taken in boiled, cooled water; however, it is important to remember that oil and water do not mix and some of the oil may be lost alongside the cup. Therefore, it is better to dilute in milk, then add water. Or, use on a sugar cube or on a lactose tablet.

Psychological and emotional support is also attributed to rose when added to a bath blend or diffused in the atmosphere. It is said to counteract a lack of cheerfulness, such as in depression and specifically with post-natal, stress-induced insomnia, a lack of concentration, reduced memory function, and stress.

Other notable uses are support for a low libido and liver congestion and protection, which is supported by the study discussed below. Cardiovascular system support has also been traditionally attributed to rose with suggested uses such as high blood pressure.

These results of a South Korean study indicate that *R. damascena* and its flavonoids may be effective to improve the cardiovascular system[4].

Notable Therapeutic Actions and Medicinal Uses

Antibacterial

IN A 2010 study 10 essential oils, namely, mint (*Mentha spicata* L., Lamiaceae), ginger (*Zingiber officinale* Rosc., Zingiberaceae), lemon (*Citrus limon* Burm.f., Rutaceae), grapefruit (*Citrus paradisi* Macf., Rutaceae), jasmine (*Jasminum grandiflora* L., Oleaceae), lavender (Mill., Lamiaceae), chamomile (*Matricaria chamomilla* L., Compositae), thyme (*Thymus vulgaris* L., Lamiaceae), rose (*Rosa damascena* Mill., Rosaceae) and cinnamon (*Cinnamomum zeylanicum* N. Lauraceae) were tested for

---

4   Kwon EK, Lee DY, Lee H, Kim DO, Baek NI, Kim YE, et al. (2010). Flavonoids from the buds of Rosa damascena inhibit the activity of 3-hydroxy-3-methylglutaryl-coenzyme a reductase and angiotensin I-converting enzyme. J Agric Food Chem., 27;58(2):882-6.

their antibacterial activities towards *Propionibacterium* acnes and *in vitro* toxicology against three human cancer cell lines. Thyme, cinnamon, and rose essential oils exhibited the best antibacterial activities towards P. acnes at a 25 percent dilution[5].

A March 2010 study also showed positive antimicrobial activity of rose against *Candida albicans* and methicillin-resistant *Staphylococcus aureus*[6].

Another study of interest in 2009 in Isparta, Turkey (where the rose industry flourishes), looked at the antioxidant and antibacterial activities of rose hydrosol, rose absolute, and distilled rose. It found rose absolute and essential oil contained high levels of phenolics and demonstrated strong antibacterial activity against Escherichia coli, Pseudomonas aeruginosa, Bacillus subtilis, Staphylococcus aureus, Chromobacterium violaceum, and Erwinia carotovora (causes decay in stored fruits and vegetables) strains[7].

Hepatic

A 1988 STUDY using rats showed rose oil provided protection for the liver. The rats had ethanol-induced liver dystrophy. At a dose of 1.01-ml/kg and 0.5-ml/kg, dystrophy and lipid infiltration were less and glycogen levels were almost completely restored. There was regeneration of liver cells. Unfortunately the botanical source of the rose oil was not given[8].

---

5   Zu, Y., Yu, H., Liang, L., Fu, Y., Efferth, T., Liu, X., et al. (2010). Activities of ten essential oils towards Propionibacterium acnes and PC-3, A-549 and MCF-7 cancer cells. Molecules, 30;15(5):3200-10.

6   Talib WH & Mahasneh AM. (2010). Antimicrobial, cytotoxicity and phytochemical screening of Jordanian plants used in traditional medicine. Molecules, 12;15(3):1811-24.

7   Ulusoy S, Boşgelmez-Tinaz G, Seçilmiş-Canbay H. (2009). Tocopherol, carotene, phenolic contents and antibacterial properties of rose essential oil, hydrosol and absolute. Curr Microbiol, 59(5):554-8. Epub 2009 Aug 18.

8   Kirov M., Burkova T., Kapurdov V., Spasovki M. (1988). Rose Oil: Lipotropic Effect in Modeled Fatty Dystrophy of the Liver. Medico Biologic Information 3:18-22.

Nervine

A 1969 STUDY using 48 medical students tested the neuro-psychic effect of rose, lavender, and geranium. The study showed an increase in concentration capacity, improved attention span, and a faster reflex action when a 1 percent solution of the oils was sprayed into the room[9].

Household Uses

IT WAS HIPPOCRATES who said, "Let food be thy medicine," and the delicious and delicate flavor of rose essential oil and hydrosol make this easy to do. Rose oil is an exquisite and luxurious addition to butter, syrup, jam, and honey. Rose water or rose hydrosol is used in desserts, pastries, and cakes. The suggested use level is 0.02-0.05-mg%*.

*The notation mg% = milligrams per 100 grams = thousandth of one percent. One mg% equals ten parts per million (10 ppm)[10]. This is a flavoring standard. Rose oil has a high level of flavoring and fragrance potential, so only very small quantities need to be used.

Perfumery

WHEN 100 PERFUMERS selected a standard for a floral aroma, Bulgarian rose was the one chosen. The absolute is unique in that it has a high tenacity alongside a deep, rosy fragrance.

Distilled rose otto has more top note, and absolute rose has more fixative power. Rose oil has a warm, deep floral, slightly spicy, rich, honey-like odor.

Rose is a very popular fragrance in many cosmetics and creams, as well as perfumes, toilet preparations, lozenges, and toothpaste.

9   Tasev T., Toleva P., Balabanova V. (1969). The neuro-psychic effect of Bulgarian rose, lavender, and geranium. Folia med, 11(5):3070317.
10   Arctander, S. (1994). Perfume and Flavor Materials of Natural Origin. Carol Stream, IL: Allured Publishing Corporation.

Rose's uplifting fragrance blends well with most other floral essential oils and it is frequently combined with jasmine. It also blends well with anise, benzoin, bergamot, black pepper, chamomile, costus, fennel, geranium, ginger, immortelle, neroli, orris root, patchouli, sandalwood, vetiver, and ylang ylang. The minimum perceptible is 0.01-0.02-mg%.

Recommended Daily Dosage (RDD)

THREE TIMES DAILY unless stated otherwise:

Adult: 1 drop three times daily on a sugar cube or lactose tablet
External: 1 to 4 drops in the bath

Cautions and Contraindications

THE TOXIC CONSTITUENT is citronellal. It is contraindicated during the first trimester of pregnancy. A 1988 study on pregnant rats showed a daily dose of 0.1-ml/kg of rose oil had no teratogenic effects on the rat embryos. At doses as high as 50% of the known LD50, there was slight toxicity to the embryo[11]. In rare cases, it may cause dermatitis. The steam-distilled rose is more suitable for internal use. The toxic rating is I[12] and a skin patch test is required.

---

11   Kirov M., Vergieva T., Spasovski M. (1988). Rose oil, mbryotoxic and Terato-genic Activity. Medico Biologic Information, 3:15-17.
12   Toxic Rating: I = Low, II = Moderate, III = High (Low Therapeutic Margin)

Rose Water Ointment

YIELDS ABOUT 9 ounces

1 ounce sweet almond oil
1/2 ounce beeswax grated
7 ounces rose water
8 drops rose oil (*Rosa damascena*)

Melt the beeswax and almond oil over a water bath. Remove from heat and cool until lukewarm. Beat in the rose water until the ointment emulsifies, and then add the 8 drops of rose essential oil.

Transfer to 9-ounce jar, label and store in a cool place. Use within 3 to 6 months.

Baby Massage Oil

YIELDS ABOUT 4 ounces

4 ounces sweet almond oil
1 to 2 drops rose oil (*Rosa damascena*)
1 to 2 drops chamomile oil (*Chamaemelum nobile*)
2 to 3 drops tangerine oil (*Citrus reticulate*)

Mix all of the oils together in a clean bottle and label. Apply as massage oil. Use with infants three months or older to support rest and relaxation.

Dorene Petersen, BA, Dip.NT, Dip.Acu, RH (AHG), *is President and Founder of the American College of Healthcare Sciences. She regularly lectures on aromatherapy and has appeared on various TV and radio shows, including Good Morning Oregon, the national radio show Voice of America, and KPTV Better Portland. Dorene's articles about aromatherapy have appeared in publications worldwide, including Alternative Therapies in Clinical Practice, The News Quarterly, Making Scents, and The Herbarist.* www.achs.edu

Waxing roses is a decorative way to preserve them.

Crafts

Making rose beads is an ancient craft; they were often used in rosaries.

Making Rose Beads, Salt-Method

Davy Dabney

USE ONLY ROSES that have not been sprayed with pesticide. Old-fashioned fragrant roses make the best beads. You can use all red roses or a mix of colors. When dry, beads will be dark red-brown.

Collect at least four quarts of opened roses. Remove the petals from the calyx. In a one gallon or larger crock layer a half inch of petals, and sprinkle about 1 teaspoon un-iodized salt over petals. Continue layering rose petals and salt until all petals are covered. Put a glass or ceramic plate (not metal) on top of petals; add a brick to weigh the petals down. After 3 to 4 days, remove the cover and stir. Re-cover and continue to stir every few days until rose petals are soft and breaking down. Some liquid from the roses will collect in the bottom of the crock.

Stir well until petals and liquid are thoroughly mixed. Use a potato masher to break down the petals into a smooth paste, about the same consistency as tomato paste. The smoother the paste, the better the beads will hold together. Place the paste into a crockpot, cover, and set temperature on low. Stir every 2 hours. If the roses are getting too dry, you may need to add several teaspoons of water. Be sure to stir well.

Keep covered, and turn the cooker off at night. Repeat until petals are smooth and of the right consistency like sugar cookie dough.

(It might take 2 or 3 days.)

When ready to make into beads, I add a teaspoon of powdered orris root for each cup of dough and a few drops of rose oil if available. Stir to blend.

Take about 1/2 cup of mixture and roll into a log about a 1/2-inch in diameter depending on the size of the finished bead you want to make. Make the bead a little larger than the finished bead needs to be, as it will shrink a bit while drying.

Pinch off about 1/2 teaspoon of the rose log and roll it around in your palms to make into a round bead. Press the bead together firmly releasing as much liquid as possible. Remember that the bead will shrink a bit as it dries. Continue making beads until you have as many as you need.

Lay out several layers of newspaper on a flat surface, such as a cookie sheet. Cut a 16-gauge wire about 18-inches long. Run the wire exactly through the middle of each bead, leaving a little space between each one so they are not touching. Let the beads dry, turning each one on the wire every day. Dry them in a warm (not hot) place. The beads are dry when they are hard to the touch.

How you design your necklace is up to you. They look best if there is another type of bead or a knot in between the rose beads.

To enhance the fragrance, put a little rose oil on your fingers as you string the beads. When not being worn, store your necklace in a small glass container with a lid to retain its fragrance.

Read *Davy Dabney*'s bio on page 201.

The Art of Waxing Roses

Theresa Loe

I FEATURED A decorative rose preservation craft in one of the herbal entertaining videos that my company produced and sold during the 1990s and, of all the crafts in my videos, it is the "waxed roses" from the video entitled "Entertaining from the Garden with Theresa Loe" that has been the most talked about, even today – almost 17 years later. The videos were VHS, (remember those?) and have long been unavailable, but the craft will never go out of style and is as special today as it was back then.

Waxed roses have endless uses – you can use them to adorn gift packages, decorate hats, embellish wreaths, topiaries and potted plants, use them as table decorations and at place settings, and more. Once waxed, these roses become very long lasting, as it can take weeks before the roses will turn brown. The paler colored pink and yellow roses will not turn brown for at least a week and the darker colored red roses stay red for much longer. Even when waxed roses turn tan and/or brown they are still very artistic looking and can be used for decoration. Flowers other than roses can be waxed using these instructions, such as Dutch Iris, Azaleas, Delphinium, Lavender, etc… Experiment! Just remember that different flowers will last differing amounts of time once they are waxed, but even a few days is great.

Tip: If using homegrown roses, try to cut them with nice long stems for ease of dipping.

Equipment

Double boiler
Candy thermometer
Ice bath

Supplies

Fresh, "full blown" or open, rose blossoms, either homegrown or store bought. Since these roses are just for decoration and not for eating, you can use florist roses. Pink, yellow and multi-colored roses tend to come out looking the best when properly waxed. White roses tend to discolor no matter what and deep red roses take on a white cast from the wax. But I encourage you to try them all and see what you like.

2 pounds paraffin wax (available in the canning section of grocery and hardware stores)
1 1/4 cups mineral oil

Remove the leaves from all of the flowers and remove any bruised outer or "guard" petals. Place the flowers to be waxed in the refrigerator for at least an hour to chill prior to waxing.

Carefully melt the 2 pounds of wax in a double boiler over low heat. Be careful; paraffin is extremely flammable!

When the wax is completely melted, remove from the heat and stir in the mineral oil. Let this mixture cool to 130° F. If the wax is too hot the flowers will burn and if it is too cool the flowers will be blotchy.

Carefully dip the chilled flowers, one at a time, into the wax using a sweeping motion. Remove from the wax and twirl slightly over the waxing mixture to remove excess and immediately dip the flower into a bowl of ice water. Let it float face down in the ice water for 10 to 15 minutes. Drain and enjoy! If you are not using the waxed roses right away for decoration or gift giving, you can store them in the refrigerator until needed. However, I like to look at the beautiful waxed flowers until I use them, so I keep them out at room temperature on my dining table or work desk. That way I can enjoy them in the meanwhile.

Note: I use an inexpensive Pyrex batter jug (mine has a nifty plastic storage lid) in a sturdy saucepan as my double boiler and I make this craft right out in the garden, with the roses, using the side burner on my grill for the heat source. I keep the prepped roses chilled in the beverage fridge we have on the patio. Couldn't be easier! When I'm done, I store the hardened mixture right in the jug, covered with the nifty lid, until I want to wax more flowers. Then I carefully re-melt the wax mixture (remembering that it already contains the mineral oil at this point) and, once it is melted and at 130 degrees, I proceed. (There is enough wax mixture that I can do this several times before making a new batch.)

Fully opened blooms are best for waxing.

Theresa Loe is a certified Master Food Preserver (aka canning expert), garden communicator (print media, video, Internet) and she is the Co-Executive Producer of the nationally televised PBS show *Growing A Greener World*, which is presently in production for its second season. Theresa and her family live and garden in the Los Angeles area of Southern California (USDA Hardiness Zone 10 - Sunset Zone 24) where she grows a myriad of roses in and among her urban homestead that includes 55 different culinary herbs and 50 different vegetables. You can read her blog by visiting her Web site www. LivingHomegrown.com.

Dried rosebuds are easily strung on wire to make wreaths or garlands.

Bios for Illustrators & Photographers

Adam Bridgewater graduated from the School of Visual Arts in 2005 with a BFA in Illustration. He won various grants and awards including the New York Fine Arts Association National Championship, New York Council for the Arts Fellowship, and received a full fellowship to the Vermont Studio Center Residency, as well as the Silas H. Rhodes Scholarship, to pursue Illustration at the School of Visual Arts. Adam has exhibited his work in two solo exhibitions and over a dozen group exhibitions, as well as publication in magazines and academic journals. He currently lives with his wife and works as a conceptual designer in Florida.

Susan Belsinger has been taking photos of roses for over 30 years, however the past two years, with this book in mind, she has gathered so many rose photos that she exceeded her memory and had to upgrade her laptop to hold them all. www.susanbelsinger.com

Pat Crocker shoots herbs, foods and gardens in all their seasons and sensuality. Her food and herb photographs illustrate her latest cookbooks, *Everyday Flexitarian* and *Preserving*. You can see examples of her work at www.PatCrocker.com.

Karen England recently broke her nifty new camera and now uses the camera in her iPhone 3Gs along with several photographic iPhone apps, most notably the "Hipstamatic App" (which was 2010 App of the Year!) to take all her garden and food photographs. She edits them using Adobe's "PhotoShop Express" app and even watermarks them using an app called "Impression". Any really great photos she prints wirelessly and directly from the camera using her inkjet printer's app for iPhone. "App"parently Karen never will need to replace her broken camera...

Donna Frawley likes to grow herbs and photograph all that grows in her garden and the food she produces from the harvest. She has created 57 culinary mixes that she sells through her business, Frawley's Fine Herbary, along with herbal tea and vinegar. She has written the *Herbal Breads Cookbook*, the *Edible Flowers Book*, *Our Favorite Recipes*, and has a DVD *Cooking with Herbs*.

Pat Kenny's first rose drawing and water coloring at the age of ten was done in May Ashcraft's backyard in Pittsburgh, Pennsylvania; she was her best friend's mother. She has been Pat's major inspiration and cheerleader all these years and she just visited the National Herb Garden with her this past summer; May is 104 years old.

Karen O'Brien, of the Green Woman's Garden, has a particular fondness for scented flowers and plants. She grows several antique rose varieties, and her daughter's middle name is, appropriately, Rose.

Dorene Petersen, President and Founder of the American College of Healthcare Sciences, travels about the globe smelling the herbs and flowers and the essential oils from these plants. She actually got to frolic in a bed of roses in Bulgaria (see page224).

Marge Powell is a plant person and an educator and finds that pictures speak a thousand words. http://www.magnoliahillsoap.com

Andrea and Matthias Reisen of Healing Spirits Herb Farm are shining examples of herbalists who walk the walk. www.healingspirit-sherbfarm.com

Kiva Rose's Web site http://bearmedicineherbals.com features her blog *The Medicine Woman's Roots* where she writes about healing herbs, harvesting, preserving and creating food and medicine from her local, native wild herbs. Her studious insight and delightful enthusiasm makes for informative and pleasurable readings.

Robert Seidel, Master Distiller since 1977, is known by some of us as the Guerilla Distiller. Check out his Web site and see his stills and his great selection of essential oils at www.essentialoil.com and his blog at guerilla-distiller.blogspot.com.

Holly H. Shimizu is always overjoyed when the roses come into full bloom in May and fill the air with their enchanting perfume – it inspires her to get the camera to try and capture some of the beauty.

Skye Suter loves to illustrate when she has half a chance! Plants (herbs in particular) and illustration are her two passions. After a career span which afforded many opportunities to indulge in both passions she is thrilled to be able to bring her work to Herb of the Year™ books.

Jane L. Taylor was the founding curator of the Michigan 4-H Children's Garden and an adjunct faculty member in the Department of Horticulture at Michigan State University. 'Betty Prior' has been one of her favorite roses. She and her husband Lee grew it in Michigan for 40+ years and now grow it in Maine.

'Seven Sisters' Rose, *Rosa multiflora platyphylla*

Photo and Illustration Credits

Front and back cover photographs: Susan Belsinger

Cover design: Heidi Lowe

Susan Belsinger: Pages, 20, 44, 48, 59, 60, 68, 74, 82, 88, 90, 98, 100, 102, 103, 104, 106, 119, 120, 128, 162, 164, 167, 168, 170, 180, 185, 198, 201, 202, 213, 215, 216, 248, color insert pages

Adam Bridgewater: Page 53

Pat Crocker: Page 94

Karen England: Pages 137, 140, 142, 145, 146, 204, 240, 247

Donna Frawley: Pages 148, 153

Pat Kenny: Pages vi, 2, 24, 73, 96, 110, 128, 154, 222, 242

Karen O'Brien: Page 88

Dorene Petersen: Pages 227, 229

Marge Powell: Pages 188, 196, 206, 251

Andrea and Matthias Reisen: Page 210

Kiva Rose: Pages 175, 176, 178

Robert Seidel: Pages 224, 239

Holly Shimizu, courtesy of the United States Botanic Garden: Pages x, 86, 87

Skye Suter: Pages 42, 67, 122, 126

Lee Taylor: Page 84

Color Insert Descriptions and Credits

Note: All page descriptions start on top left corner of page and go clockwise from there.

Page 1

'Pat Austin' rose in the garden at USBG, Washington, D.C.; Holly Shimizu, courtesy of the United Sates Botanic Garden.

Page 2

Wild woodland rose on the hiking trail at the Ozark Folk Center, Mountain View, Arkansas; Susan Belsinger.

Signage describes how the roses are categorized and sold at Antique Rose Emporium, San Antonio, Texas; Susan Belsinger.

Gorgeous pink, long-lasting 'Betty Prior' in bloom at the USBG, Washington, D.C.; Holly Shimizu, courtesy of the United States Botanic Garden.

'Yankee Doodle' in the Rose Garden at Dow Gardens in Midland, Michigan; Susan Belsinger.

Page 3

Wild rose hips (*R. rugosa*) taken by the beach near Newport, Rhode Island; Susan Belsinger.

'Minorcan' is the local name for 'Louis Phillipe' in Callahan, Florida; Marge Powell.

Rose-covered cottage, *Lisin na Cre*, West County Cork, Ireland; Susan Belsinger.

'Mister Lincoln' is a handsome red rose in the Rose Garden at Dow Gardens in Midland, Michigan; Susan Belsinger.

This pass-along rose planted by Ida Branscomb covers the Herb Cabin at the Ozark Folk Center, Mountain View, Arkansas; Susan Belsinger.

Page 4

This pink, hybrid, bush-type rose was in Jeanne and Rob Calkin's backyard when they moved into their home in Midland, Michigan; Susan Belsinger.

'Thomas Affleck' is a popular, bright, dark pink rose at Antique Rose Emporium, San Antonio, Texas; Susan Belsinger.

Pale pink and perfect 'Heritage' rose at the USBG, Washington, D.C.; Holly Shimizu, courtesy of the United States Botanic Garden.

'Baronne Prevost' wows with its many-petaled, double, dark pink blooms, Mendon, Massachusetts; Karen O'Brien.

'Color Magic' hybrid tea rose in the Rose Garden at Dow Gardens in Midland, Michigan; Susan Belsinger.

The unusual 'Moonstone' rose is in the Rose Garden at Dow Gardens in Midland, Michigan; Susan Belsinger.

This pink beauty was taken at Abele Greenhouse in Saginaw, Michigan; Susan Belsinger.

Beloved *Rosa rugosa*, Mendon, Massachusetts; Karen O'Brien.

Page 5

Teatime with black tea with rose petals, dried rose hips and Rose Petal Honey, Little Rock, Arkansas; Susan Belsinger.

Amb-ROSE-ia fruit salad with rose petals, Encinitas, California; Karen England.

Rose Petal Freezer Jam, Encinitas, California; Karen England.

Infusing rose petals in vinegar, Brookeville, Maryland; Susan Belsinger.

Baby Greens and Edible Flower Salad, Brookeville, Maryland; Susan Belsinger.

Rose Petal Honey, Brookeville, Maryland; Susan Belsinger.

Page 6

Floribunda 'Orangeade' is brilliant in the Rose Garden at Dow Gardens in Midland, Michigan; Susan Belsinger.

'Livin Easy' is a showstopper at the Antique Rose Emporium, San Antonio, Texas; Susan Belsinger.

'Strike it Rich' grandiflora rose in the Rose Garden at Dow Gardens in Midland, Michigan; Susan Belsinger.

'Carding Hill'™ at Abele Greenhouse in Saginaw, Michigan; Susan Belsinger.

'Julia Child', Bellingrath Gardens, Alabama; Pat Crocker.

Beautiful bi-colored rose in Crystal Kauer's rose garden, Saginaw, Michigan; Susan Belsinger.

Page 7

Assorted, multi-colored rose petals, Brookeville, Maryland; Susan Belsinger.

Home-distillation of rose petals, Encinitas, California; Karen England.

Pink rose petals infused in vodka, Brookeville, Maryland; Susan Belsinger.

Many-colored rose blooms, Brookeville, Maryland; Susan Belsinger.

Rose-petal essence and rose water, Brookeville, Maryland; Susan Belsinger.

Healing Spirits Herb Farm products, Rose Glycerite and Flower Essence, Brookeville, Maryland; Susan Belsinger.

Page 8

Waxed roses, Encinitas, California; Karen England.

Rose bud wreath made by Sherri Byrne of The Herb Cupboard in Fort Plain, New York, taken in Brookeville, Maryland; Susan Belsinger.

Rose bud garland and sachets filled with rose and lavender created by Sherri Byrne and dried Bulgarian rose buds, taken in Little Rock, Arkansas; Susan Belsinger.

Basket of rose petals, India; Dorene Petersen.

Rose bead necklace created by the Potomac Unit of the HSA, Brookeville, Maryland; Susan Belsinger.

Counted-cross stitch of fairy and roses by Sherryl Buck, Midland, Michigan; Susan Belsinger.

Herb of the Year™ Selection

How the Herb of the Year™ is Selected

Every year since 1995, the International Herb Association has chosen an Herb of the Year to highlight. The Horticultural Committee evaluates possible choices based on their being outstanding in at least two of the three major categories: medicinal, culinary, or decorative. Many other herb organizations support the herb of the year selection and we work together to educate the public about these herbs during the year.

Herbs of the Year™: Past, Present and Future:

1995 Fennel
1996 Monarda
1997 Thyme
1998 Mint
1999 Lavender
2000 Rosemary
2001 Sage
2002 Echinacea
2003 Basil
2004 Garlic
2005 Oregano & Marjoram
2006 Scented Geraniums
2007 Lemon Balm
2008 Calendula
2009 Bay Laurel
2010 Dill
2011 Horseradish
2012 Rose
2013 Elderberry
2014 Artemisia
2015 Savory

Join the IHA

ASSOCIATE WITH OTHER herb businesses and like-minded folks, network and have fun while you are doing it!

Membership Levels:

$500	Sponsor
$100	Business/Professional
$25	Additional member from your business
$100	Individual/Hobbyist
$25	Full-time Student
$50	Educator
$50	Small Business Start-up (first year of membership)

Log onto www.iherb.org to see what we are all about!

Membership includes:

Your business information listed on www.iherb.org
Membership directory
Herb of the Year publication
Quarterly newsletters
Online herbal support
Discounts on conference fees
Promotional support for IHA's Herb of the Year program and National Herb Week
Support for National Herb Day
Association with a network of diverse herbal businesses

Recipe Index